Praise for This Book:

"Don't hire anyone without first reading this book. Alexandra Levit offers both tactical and strategic advice regarding not just the function of hiring but its radial impacts. It's impossible to pick up *Success for Hire* and NOT discover multiple ways to improve your current hiring process—no matter how good it is."

—Francie Dalton, President, Dalton Alliances, Inc.

"Alexandra Levit has written a highly informative book, which strikes a perfect balance in providing specific best practices and checklists, while also inspiring readers to think more broadly and creatively about their human capital challenges. Anyone who is responsible for recruiting, staffing, and developing high-performing employees and managers, no matter how senior or experienced, will benefit from the wisdom that has been collected and synthesized so masterfully."

—Ben Dattner, Professor of Industrial and Organizational Psychology,
New York University

"*Success for Hire* is an excellent guide for anyone concerned about attracting and retaining great talent. It is a comprehensive compilation of leading contemporary talent practices. . . a one-stop resource for developing strategies to ensure your organization has the talent needed to succeed."

—Bob Paxton, Vice President of Human Resources, Whirlpool Corporation

"Alexandra Levit has given us an informed, well-written, and comprehensive overview of how to attract, motivate, and retain top-performers. In today's complex, dynamic, and global economy, she has given leaders at all organizational levels a practical roadmap to fulfill their most important mandate—leveraging their talent."

—Todd Harris, Ph.D., Director of Research, PI Worldwide

"An easy and enjoyable read, *Success for Hire* provides a fool-proof, step-by-step guide for companies to attract great people. This is a great resource for human resource departments to develop a plan for hiring and retaining associates. Alexandra Levit guides us through the entire employee life cycle with suggestions and solutions that are practical, easy to apply, and make a lot of sense."

—John Uprichard, President, Find Great People International

"The days of placing an ad in the local paper or on a big online job site and quickly finding a great candidate are gone. History. The war for talent is in full swing and only those organizations who take a strategic approach—backed up with strong processes and relationships—will win. *Success for Hire* should be mandatory reading for all managers and HR professionals. Alexandra Levit does an outstanding job of emphasizing the most important actions you can take to improve the quality and retention of your new hires."

—Lisa Haneberg, Management Consultant and Author of *Organization Development Basics, 10 Steps to Be a Successful Manager,* and *Developing Great Managers* (ASTD Press)

"*Success for Hire* is an easy-to-use guide offering cutting-edge and innovative strategies for selecting and keeping outstanding employees. It is not your typical 'How to Hire' book, but instead provides real world tips from experts in the field, case studies, and worksheets to guide you. It's a perfect refresher for all involved in the hiring process and an excellent risk-management tool."

—Judith Brown, HR Specialist, McNeil Technologies, Inc.

Success for Hire

Success for Hire

Simple Strategies to Find and Keep Outstanding Employees

Alexandra Levit

Alexandria, Virginia

ASTD Press is an internationally renowned source of insightful and practical information on workplace learning and performance topics, including training basics, evaluation and return on investment, instructional systems development, e-learning, leadership, and career development.

Ordering information: Books published by ASTD Press can be purchased by visiting our website at store.astd.org or by calling 800.628.2783 or 703.683.8100.

Library of Congress Control Number: 2007931357

ISBN-10: 1-56286-504-8
ISBN-13: 978-1-56286-504-7

ASTD Press Editorial Staff:
Director: Cat Russo
Manager, Acquisitions & Editorial Relations: Mark Morrow
Editorial Manager: Jacqueline Edlund-Braun
Editorial Assistant: Maureen Soyars
Retail Trade Manager: Yelba Quinn
Copyeditor: Alfred F. Imhoff
Indexer: April Davis
Proofreader: Kris Patenaude
Interior Design and Production: Kathleen Schaner
Cover Design: Ana Ilieva
Cover Illustration: Nicholas Eveleigh

Printed by Victor Graphics, Inc., Baltimore, Maryland, www.victorgraphics.com

Contents

Acknowledgements

I would like to take this opportunity to thank the individuals who contributed to making *Success for Hire* the best title it could be. I couldn't have done it without the dozens of organizations, professionals, consultants, managers, and authors who generously shared their hiring and retention expertise and best practices, or the publicists who put me in touch with them and facilitated their participation.

Thanks to the incredibly hard-working team at ASTD Press, including Mark Morrow, Jacqueline Edlund-Braun, Yelba Quinn, and Alfred Imhoff, for shepherding the book from a pea of an idea to a finished product we're all proud of.

Special appreciation goes out to Lisa Haneberg, a role model of mine who first suggested I write for ASTD, my agents Alex Glass and Michelle Wolfson, David Dunne and my team at Edelman, Doug Conant, Penelope Trunk, and Bruce Tulgan for inspiring me this year, and, most important, my always-supportive husband, Stewart Shankman.

Preface

In my almost 10 years as a marketing communications consultant and career coach to some of the most recognizable companies in the world, I've learned that every organization—from the free-wheeling startup to the gentle *Fortune* 500 giant—faces challenges when it comes to attracting and retaining the best employees.

The forthcoming labor shortage brought on by the Baby Boomers' retirement is making many human resources professionals and managers scramble to do things "the right way" after years of improvisation. They understand that they'll need to replace Baby Boomers with members of the more fastidious Millennial Generation—those currently in their 20s and early 30s whose loyalty lies with their own career growth. If organizations don't master best practices for hiring and retention now, market superiority and industry competitiveness will simply pass them by as the Millennials and their life-balance-oriented older siblings in Generation X go elsewhere.

During my employment at a top communications firm and global software company, no one set out to properly recruit and retain me, and as I became schooled in the ways of the 21st-century business world, I copied my managers' fly-by-the-seat-of-our-pants techniques for candidate searches, interviewing, and training. Although I considered myself a good judge of character, as a supervisor I experienced as much turnover as anyone. As the saying goes, "You don't know what you don't know." And when I started to research this book and began lining up material from dozens of experts who could weigh in on today's cutting-edge recruitment and retention strategies, I had no idea just how much I was about to learn.

The act of writing this book—which often prompted me to challenge conventional wisdom, look for ways that technology could make a given process more efficient, and seek out little-known but proven formulas that would allow me to make the right hiring and resource decisions nearly all the time—really has made me smarter. I hope that reading it does the same for you.

Alexandra Levit
April 2008

Introduction

Dodge Recruitment Disasters and Win the War for Talent

When have you seen

- a senior vice president who charmed the pants off the executive leadership team during a dinner out, only to turn into a monster when faced with managing subordinates?
- a midlevel account executive whose vast industry knowledge impressed everyone, until he came to work and couldn't seem to apply that knowledge to getting his own job done?
- a top-notch branch manager candidate who was lost to the competition because the interviewer forgot to follow up?
- a bright and ambitious college grad who left after a month because the organization wasn't at all what she expected?

Much as it pains us to admit it, we've all witnessed situations like these, whether we've been in the work world for three years or 30 years. Maybe we've even played an instrumental role in these kinds of situations. It's certainly not for a lack of good intentions. We obviously understand that hiring good people is critical to our business success. It's just that in the midst of a pressure-filled working environment with dozens of competing priorities, we've failed to follow the steps that make effective recruitment and retention of top talent a reality.

Researchers at the University of Michigan have found that the way the typical job interview is conducted increases the likelihood of choosing the best candidate by less than 2 percentage points. Other mistakes we make that result in poor hiring decisions include

- not thinking about who and what you need, and why you need them
- not knowing how and where to recruit top talent
- not having a defined selection process that candidates can move through seamlessly
- not having a means to objectively analyze candidates
- not leveraging the latest technology to increase recruiting efficiencies and improve the organization's ability to retain employees
- not carefully checking résumés and references
- not screening or testing candidates to determine important traits or skills
- not being upfront with candidates during the recruitment process
- not taking the time to make the best possible first impression with new hires
- not paying attention to candidates' training, development, and overall needs after the hire.

Employment projections from the U.S. Bureau of Labor Statistics have determined that as early as 2010, when the Baby Boomers start retiring en masse, there won't be enough workers available to staff the nation's jobs. Your challenge will be to employ the right mix of people and resources to ensure that the best employees find, choose, and then stay in your organization. This book was written with one goal in mind: to provide a concrete, practical, easy-to-implement road map for undertaking an effective hiring process that will help you remain competitive in the talent-hungry 21st century. The book is designed for busy hiring managers and human resources professionals, and it progresses logically, chapter by chapter, through these steps:

Chapter 1: Analyze Your Required Positions. In this chapter, you'll learn how to carefully assess the jobs you need to fill, and how to gain advance buy-in from everyone who's part of the hiring process.

Chapter 2: Search for the Best Candidates. This chapter explores how to develop a well-rounded, multifaceted sourcing strategy that results in a higher percentage of qualified leads and less time spent interviewing candidates.

Chapter 3: Narrow the Field of Applicants. Here, we'll discuss how to use web-based technology to ensure the proper filtering of application materials.

Chapter 4: Create a Strategy for Interviewing. In this chapter, you'll learn how to prepare in advance for interviews, create a standardized meeting format, ask the right questions, and employ work simulations.

Chapter 5: Do Effective Background Research. This chapter discusses best practices for calling candidates' references, conducting background checks and credential verifications, and administering valid personality and skill assessments.

Chapter 6: Make the Job Offer. In this chapter, you'll learn the mechanics behind making an official job offer, including the materials you'll want to send to showcase your organization and the advantages and disadvantages of using an employment contract.

Chapter 7: Improve New Hire Orientation. This chapter shows you how to increase your retention rates by 25 percent by designing your orientation program in a way that drives forward a new employee's successful acclimation into your business.

Chapter 8: Develop Strong Training and Growth Plans. This chapter guides you in current offerings, developing workable course designs, customizing programs according to individual employee needs, and facilitating mentoring.

Chapter 9: Achieve Long-Term Retention. This chapter equips you to ensure that your best people stay put and shows you how to provide growth opportunities and incentives, promote work/life balance, and encourage more effective supervisor/employee relationships.

In the nine chapters ahead, we'll look at how companies are using innovative methods to achieve their recruitment and retention objectives, and we'll hear from experts who have learned what works and what doesn't. Throughout, there are many quotations from interviews with these experts, along with citations and quotations from useful books and articles (you'll find full information on these and other works in the references and suggested reading sections at the end of the book). Each chapter also includes worksheets, sample documents, and sidebar stories to help you optimize your organization's recruitment and retention process. The book concludes with an afterword.

Forgetting about the organization for a second, by learning the best recruitment and retention techniques available, you'll serve your own career well—because when the people you hire succeed, you do as well!

Analyze Your Required Positions: Forethought Trumps Knee-Jerk Every Time

.... **In this chapter, you'll learn to** ....

- define the business requirements for a given position
- understand your organizational culture
- create a written job analysis
- convene a committee of stakeholders to finalize a job description

Developing a sound hiring process and using it for every new hire makes sense in theory, but what happens when you come into the office one morning at 8 a.m. and find yourself staring at the resignation letter of your top sales executive or marketing manager? Your knee-jerk reaction is to do whatever it takes to fill the position immediately, before the departure has a severe impact on operations. "But rushing into a new relationship can block your intuition, destroy your objectivity, and be a professional landmine," says John Uprichard (2006) of Find Great People International in "How to Avoid Making a Panic Hire." "Every executive can tell horror stories about split-second recruiting decisions, where time and energy are drained on the wrong applicant and money is lost in the process."

In the midst of panic, one of the first things managers neglect is the first stage of the hiring process: the job analysis. This is because people tend to think that if the position has been occupied before, things like requisite skills, responsibilities, and performance criteria should be obvious. In fact, many firms never take the time to study what a job specifically entails; instead, they rely on institutional knowledge and subjective opinions of what a person is supposed to do in a certain role at a certain level. They also fail to take into account the possibility that a previously occupied job might need to be changed to meet the evolving needs of the firm or department.

Finding the right candidate for a job is much easier when you take the time to carefully analyze the job you need to fill, and when everyone who is part of the hiring process agrees in advance on a set of criteria. "Instead of looking for the right person to fill the open position, organizations should start with the end goal in mind and work backwards," says Tom Gimbel, founder and CEO of the LaSalle Network, a staffing and recruiting firm. "You start by creating a perfect, 100 percent picture of the skills, experience, and personality the successful candidate will have, and then strive to attract and retain candidates with at least 80 percent." Let's take a look at how that "100 percent picture" is developed.

Creating the 100 Percent Picture: Defining Business Requirements

The first step in creating the 100 percent picture of the successful candidate is to determine your business requirements for the position, in the context of the overall company landscape. What are the core products, services, initiatives, and financial circumstances that will have an impact on this new hire? In filling this position, what are you hoping to achieve? What are the business problems the new hire will need to solve in the first 90 days or the first year, and what major projects will he or she need to complete? Who will be the key players in this new hire's work life, including supervisors, colleagues, reports, other departments, customers, and partners?

Next, you'll want to do some in-house interviewing. Your mission? To uncover a profile of the top performer in the position you're looking to fill. Talk with and observe in action those who are already doing excellent work in the same or similar jobs, and/or get input from the person you're replacing on the traits, skills, behaviors, attitudes, and experience that make him or her successful. For a broader perspective, encourage co-workers who have worked with those who've held the open position in the past to share their thoughts on the behaviors that were most and least valuable on the job.

Assessing Your Culture: Fish Discover Water Last

To create the 100 percent picture of the successful candidate, you also need to understand the role your unique corporate culture plays in devising your selection criteria. However, insiders rarely have an objective view of their culture or business. As Steve Springer (2006), author of *Stop Hiring Failures*, puts it: "Fish discover water last, so you should consider finding an external advisor who will ask the tough questions, interview key employees, and create an accurate, objective assessment of your company's work environment, values, and style." This person, who can be an executive recruiter, an attorney, or vendor, should interview employees at several levels of the organization to gain insights about how things are done in your culture. Questions should explore areas such as management style and practices, customer relations, attitudes toward quality, and the willingness of management to involve employees in decision making.

Experts in job analysis believe that a large emphasis should be placed on organizational culture. "Recognize that jobs do not exist in a vacuum but are instead imbedded in a social system," says David Hyatt, president of CorVirtus, a corporate culture and human resources consulting and research firm. "Hiring professionals are beginning to realize that an effort should be made to hire employees who not only possess the requisite skills, knowledge, and attributes but also fit with the organization's culture and values. Thus it is important that this culture is defined and documented in the job analysis process."

An outside consultant may also be useful in soliciting information from internal and external contacts regarding their needs and perceptions of the ideal potential candidate. The consultant would also be in a better position to speak to past employees who have been unsuccessful in the position and learn about the reasons behind their failures. You never know—they might give you an earful that helps to explain why you're experiencing turnover in that particular job. Some factors, including departmental conflicts, inadequate training, and ineffective management, may be things you should look to remedy as part of the hiring process.

Creating Your Targeted Job Analysis

The next step in creating the 100 percent picture of the successful candidate is to use the information you glean from these interviews to create a written job analysis (figure 1-1), which you will later pare down into a final job description (figure 1-2). You will need to list the major, everyday duties of the position in question. Focus on the typical problems the potential employee might face, and what measurable results he or she will be expected to achieve. When it comes to education, you'll want to differentiate between what's essential and what's preferable. Candidates are more likely to lie about their education than any other aspect of their background, so if a certain degree or certification is absolutely necessary, you will need to have a system in place for verifying credentials.

As for required experience, Martin Yate (2006) says in his book *Hiring the Best*:

> If you demand five years of solid experience, quantify what it is that people will be able to deliver as a result of that experience that a candidate with only three years could not. It's one thing to say that you need someone with 15 years of manufacturing experience, it's another to expect the employee to run a 24/7 four-shift operation and then move it to the Philippines in 15 months.

Yate also suggests that there is a group of behaviors that are common to all professionals in the successful execution of jobs at all levels and in all professions. In developing your job analysis, you should emphasize those behaviors that are key to successful project execution within your organizational culture, including:

- effective written and verbal communication
- time management and organization
- team orientation and collaborative spirit
- high energy level
- high motivation level
- analytical and problem-solving skills
- confidence
- reliability and personal commitment
- honesty and integrity
- pride and attention to detail

- dedication and learning orientation
- goal and profit orientation
- efficiency.

When considering the professional behaviors that will be most valuable for your new hire to exhibit, you'll also want to take into account your own style as a manager. In "Finding the Right Person at the Right Time," Chris Musselwhite (2007)—the CEO of Discovery Learning, an organization that develops experiential, hands-on learning

Figure 1-1. Job Analysis Worksheet

Date _____

Prepared by _____

Title _____

Department _____

Job Title _____ **Reports to** _____

General Business Landscape

Objectives of Position

Critical Duties and Projects

Key Results and Deliverables

Skills Required

Professional Behaviors Required

Potential Issues Faced

Resources Required

Figure 1-2. Job Description

Date _____

Prepared by _____

Title _____

Department _____

Job Title _____   **Reports to** _____

Job Summary

Salary Range and Benefits

Developmental Track

Major Duties

1.
2.
3.
4.

Minimum Educational Requirements

1.
2.
3.
4.

Minimum Skills Requirements and Work Experience

1.
2.
3.
4.

Personality Traits and/or Management Style

1.
2.
3.
4.

Key Relationships

Number and Titles of People Supervised:

People Authorized to Assign Work:

Regular, On-the-Job Contacts:

Special Considerations

1.
2.
3.
4.

---

and personal assessment tools—maintains that self-awareness is a hallmark of all great leaders. Understanding your personal problem-solving and decision-making process is critical to knowing how any new employee will complement your strengths and cover your weaknesses. One good way to get essential insight into your management style is with personality self-assessments, such as the Myers-Briggs Type Indicator and the Change Style Indicator. You can also use 360-degree multi-rater leadership surveys that provide feedback from supervisors, peers, and reports.

Reaching Consensus: Convening the Committee

Once you've compiled an initial job analysis, the next step in creating the 100 percent picture of the successful candidate is to select a committee that will assist you in making the hiring decision. The committee, which will consist of three to five stakeholders, should provide feedback on the job analysis. In your first meeting, recommends Steve Springer, you should also discuss the number and level of people supervised, decision authority, scope of projects, developmental track, and special considerations such as technical and physical requirements and travel and relocation.

Now, using your interview notes and your job analysis as a base, select as a group the four most critical knowledge areas, skills, and attributes (known as KSAs) and work experiences the candidate should have already obtained. Also agree upon the four most essential educational attainments and four most desirable personality traits based on the vacant position and its place within your culture. Finalize your selections in a written job description (figure 1-2), making sure that every member of the group understands the meaning behind each item and is on the same page regarding exactly what you're looking for. It's critical that all the relevant stakeholders reach a consensus on what exactly the job is now, before the recruitment process begins. "Otherwise," says Ben Dattner, professor of industrial and organizational psychology and organizational effectiveness consultant, "stakeholders may dispute the qualifications of given candidates as a way of trying to steer the position in the direction they want it to go. For example, if some people see the chief financial officer role as primarily a financial management role, they may want to hire certain candidates, while others may view the chief financial officer as primarily a strategic role and therefore will prefer other candidates. It can be costly to the organization and annoying to candidates if disputes about what the position is are not resolved ahead of time."

As you look ahead to interviewing, it's helpful to take your job description and rank the five to seven most important items on it in priority order. At this stage, it's also appropriate for you and your colleagues to outline how to sell the opportunity and your company's value proposition to the highly desirable candidate you're hoping to attract. This will come in handy in adapting your job descriptions to job advertisements, and in second and third interviews when the pressure is on to seal the deal. Additionally, you may want to get input from your committee on the upcoming candidate search. Dora Vell, CEO of the retained executive search firm Vell & Associates, recommends discussing the sources to target and the sources to avoid, the group that should interview candidates, the timeframe for bringing a new hire onboard, and the compensation package that will be offered.

Show Me the Money: The True Value of Job Analysis

Although we've outlined a specific process here, there's no single approach that will result in a successful job analysis. "There are multiple ways to gather and analyze job information," says David Hyatt. "You can use job observations, interviews with job incumbents and supervisors, review of organizational information, and structured questionnaires. Any one of these methods by itself may be flawed, but jointly they should converge on the true nature of the job. For example, job incumbents may present an exaggerated representation of their job during an interview, but by actually observing their job performance, you'll obtain a more realistic picture. Still, the job incumbent interview can provide insights (qualifications needed, mental processes, and the like) that cannot be gleaned through observations alone."

A multiple-method, thorough, and systematic job analysis is also essential to ensure the legal defensibility of your hiring processes. "You have to be able to justify the steps in your hiring process, such as assessments and interviews, as job-related and valid, and you can't do that if you don't have a clear understanding of the job," says Lisa Harpe, a senior consultant with the Peopleclick Research Institute, a division of Peopleclick, a talent acquisition solution provider. "Some companies, for instance, ask hiring managers to document specific job requirements every time they have an opening, so you could have multiple job descriptions for the same position. This would compromise your ability to evaluate your recruiting and hiring processes and will increase your vulnerability to claims of disparate treatment, since different candidates for the same job could be held to different standards."

Completed job analyses have useful applications beyond the hiring process. According to Maren Franklin (2005), the author of the *ASTD InfoLine Guide to Job Analysis*, the results can be leveraged for many purposes, including determining tasks for new hires to learn, assessing training or continuing education needs, focusing on select tasks to streamline processes and procedures, analyzing the value of positions, and reorganizing roles to meet shifting business needs. Take the time to experiment and determine the approach that will serve your organization best in the long term. For more on how job analyses work in practice, see the sidebar.

Thought you'd just skip the job analysis? Experts report why that's not a smart approach. Let's hear directly from some people with wisdom on this:

Chris Musselwhite, CEO, Discovery Learning:

> Our company is small, and people work very closely. Because of the respect we have for each other, we work effectively through conflict in a way that suits our team and defines our low key, easygoing culture. A while back, I had the opportunity to hire a person who had the perfect résumé to bring an entirely new and attractive skill set to our team. Although her reputation was not one that would've been seen to mesh with our group, I ignored that and hired her based on her skill set. It was a mistake. She was very confrontational and didn't like working closely

Scottsdale Insurance Case Study

When Scottsdale Insurance decided to reorganize to better meet customer needs, its managers recognized that new positions would need to be created and existing responsibilities modified. Given that a large percentage of the work in any insurance company lies with underwriting, this was an obvious place to start. The decision to create a new marketing function, including product director roles, surfaced a two-part question:

1. What, exactly, were associates in existing underwriting positions doing today?
2. What, if anything, would be changed with the creation of the new product director positions?

Although job descriptions existed for underwriters, specific daily tasks varied by line of business (product) and by underwriter level. A comprehensive picture of the current role was necessary to decide what underwriters would do in the future structure. Job analysis was conducted on the underwriter positions for four different lines of business. Top performers representing all four lines of business participated in separate sessions and then were brought together in one large session to synchronize task statements and coordinate job analysis results. Each group invested approximately 12 total hours in the analysis process. The job analysis results were compiled into one job map for management to analyze and use in making decisions about which tasks would remain the underwriters' responsibility and which tasks would become the responsibility of the newly created positions. This data spun off into a separate job design process for the new positions, providing a foundation of duties and tasks. The analysis also resulted in two other significant developments. Underwriter tasks originally not common to all four lines of business became the target of training efforts to ensure that all underwriters have the knowledge areas, skills, and attributes to perform in the newly structured role. Also, tasks that are common to all but are executed differently became the focus of task analysis and of process and procedure streamlining.

Management in other divisions of Scottsdale took interest in the work done in underwriting and began the job analysis process for their own areas. As in underwriting, results will be used as a foundation to improve job functions, work processes, and associates' knowledge areas, skills, and abilities.

This case study was provided by ASTD Infoline (Franklin 2005).

with others. In the end, it didn't matter how qualified she was, because she simply could not work with our team. The lesson: Consider your culture and hire based on your cultural needs as well as your organization's skill needs.

Francie Dalton, president, Dalton Alliances:

A particular candidate had a stunning reputation as being brilliant at X and had repeatedly distinguished himself in the X arena. Solely because of his reputation regarding X, a company hired him to do X, Y, and Z. Blinded by the "star quality" of this person, the hiring organization made no effort whatsoever to assess his strengths regarding Y and Z functions, which were ultimately revealed to be so deficient as to necessitate an expensive restructuring.

Terry Laudal, senior vice president of human resources, SAP America:

I remember a situation where we had a senior executive join our company after a series of interviews. We were all concerned about the culture shift for this person to move from a slow, bureaucratic work environment to one with a lightning-fast pace, driven by quick decision making and responsiveness. This candidate convinced us, after some preliminary prodding, that he would have no problem making the shift. So we brought him onboard. Approximately three weeks later, he came to me and said he was really struggling with the pace and the speed in which things moved, that he had not anticipated the drastic switch, and that he was no longer confident he could make the change required. The lesson learned is that selection is a tough business, and we must balance our need to move quickly with high-quality selection techniques.

Kevin Fleming, president and CEO, Effective Executive Coaching ("the Inc. shrink"):

I once served as an executive coach to an ever-growing engineering firm that had very little understanding of EQ [emotional intelligence] and its relation to success. I was assisting in the assessment of candidates for a new CEO and there was indeed a "rising star" who left all the candidates in the dust. However, his technical competence, while impressive, had nothing to do with the job description of a CEO, and his gregariousness and sociability, which meant everything to the Board, was not actually as important at the C level, where being authentic is more critical than being liked. When I pointed these things out, I was unfortunately vetoed, a decision the company later regretted.

Sandy Gross, managing partner, Pinetum Partners:

The participants at one company couldn't agree on the criteria needed to hire but engaged in a search anyway, hoping that they would figure it out over time as they saw candidates. The recruiting firm had a broad and somewhat undefined idea of what the client was looking for and ended up interviewing a lot of candidates, spending time coaching the candidates to get them ready for the interview(s), obtaining feedback from the client, and presenting it to the candidates. The candidates in turn spent time preparing for the interview, getting knowledgeable about the hiring company, and taking time away from their present job. Many people were involved in communicating back and forth to figure out where things stood, all the while keeping the candidates hopeful. The search went on for quite some time, and the marketplace started to wonder why the company was having a hard time filling the position, which made future candidates hesitant to get involved.

Making It Happen

Finding the right candidate is much easier when you take the time to carefully analyze the job you need to fill, and everyone who is part of the hiring process agrees in advance on a set of criteria. Make sure you:

- Conduct in-house interviewing to uncover a profile of the top performer in the position you're looking to fill.
- Understand the role that your unique corporate culture plays in devising your selection criteria.
- Use the information you glean from your interviews to create a written job analysis by listing everyday duties, typical problems, and anticipated results for the position.
- Convene a committee of stakeholders to finalize a job description.

Search for the Best Candidates: Your Talent Is Out There, If You Know Where to Look

In this chapter, you'll learn to

- use internal recruiting to your best advantage
- write effective job advertisements and online content
- leverage networking activities to develop a comprehensive sourcing strategy
- determine when and how to employ professional search firms.

Now that you have a clear understanding of the job you're recruiting for, it's time to scout out the best candidates. In most organizations, sourcing strategies are undertaken jointly by hiring managers and human resources professionals and involve the use of a variety of channels. For instance, one recruiter I spoke to recently, who worked for a consumer packaged goods company, said that his efforts to bring onboard a new chief marketing officer included an ad in the *Wall Street Journal*, postings on 6figurejobs.com and the American Marketing Association's website, participation in an executive networking event sponsored by the Business Marketing Association, and a targeted engagement with an executive search firm.

A well-rounded, multifaceted talent search will result in a much higher percentage of qualified leads and less time spent interviewing candidates who aren't a smart fit for the job or the organization. In this chapter, we'll identify the best ways to locate strong matches for your open positions, starting with the most basic and often most successful of recruiting strategies: hiring from within.

Internal Recruitment: Risk Less with a Proven Entity

The last time I was job hunting, one mantra I heard over and over was that most job openings aren't advertised because organizations prefer to fill positions with individuals already working for the company. If you think about it, this makes sense. Existing employees are known entities. As Steve Springer (2006) says in his book *Stop Hiring Failures*, "Outside recruits always emphasize their strengths, talents, and successes, but generally fail to divulge their shortcomings or failures. With insiders, you know their limitations."

Starting your search inside your own walls serves an additional purpose. You'll show that you care about your current employees by giving them a first crack at opportunities to grow their careers and by rewarding them for putting forth qualified candidates from within their own personal and professional networks. List postings on your firm's intranet a few weeks before you begin the external search, and make it clear to employees that it's both acceptable and encouraged to apply for another job inside the organization. Make sure, however, that internal candidates understand the rules associated with a transfer—for example, to be considered, an employee must be in good standing with his or her current manager and must have been employed with the company for at least a year. You can also take advantage of your people's industry contacts by setting up an employee referral program. According to Christopher Pritchard (2007), the author of *101 Strategies for Recruiting Success*, a well-run program will

- provide clear and concise instructions to employees and applicants
- time stamp submissions to avoid duplication among employees
- follow up with the employee in a timely manner
- maintain an organized referral tracking system
- offer employee incentives (often a monetary bonus) that are tied to a clearly defined retention period for the new hire (often six months to a year).

Pritchard cautions against dropping the ball and failing to follow up with employee referrals. "Since many employees refer friends, this could turn into an employee relations nightmare," he says. The same follow-up rules, by the way, apply to employees seeking internal positions themselves.

A new spin on the employee referral program is the alumni referral program, an initiative in which you reward people who have left your organization on good terms when they refer contacts to you. Keep in contact with your alumni through a newsletter or website and provide them with incentives similar to those for current employees should one of their recommendations be hired.

Make Your Job Ads Sing

We now move to external recruiting strategies, the first of which is straight advertising. Many organizations still use print ads, in particular to solicit applications, but this type of advertising isn't something you should engage in just because "we've always done it that way." Rather, vehicles for print ads should be considered carefully based on the industry and the type, level, and geographic location of the position. For example, if you're recruiting for a low-level customer service job, you might place ads in your local newspaper and penny saver publication, but if your open position is for a midlevel software engineer who would be willing to relocate, an ad in a national industry publication like *Computerworld* or *Information Week* might be a better bet.

The publications you choose will help ensure that you attract the right audiences for your opening, and now you must craft a strong message that will resonate with those individuals. In his book *Hiring the Best*, author Martin Yate (2006) offers the following tips for writing an attention-grabbing job ad:

- The headline should be witty, promote qualities that are likely to appeal to the reader, and mention the job title. Sample headlines: "Executive Administrator to the CEO: The Core of the Executive Team"; "Financial Stock Administrator: Right Place, Right Time."
- The body copy should excite the reader by talking about what the new hire will be doing rather than what experience is necessary.
- The more must-haves you put in an ad, the more potential respondents you will lose. Recruitment ads draw best when they are specific enough to

whet the appetite to know more but vague enough to keep people from ruling themselves out.

- Use your ads as a public relations vehicle to send the message that your organization is a progressive, professional place to work.
- Never use a gender-specific structure. Talk in terms of "you."
- Ads that do not include some mention of remuneration are thought to get only half the response rate of ads that do mention money.
- Options for contact not only increase response; they also keep you on the right side of the law.

See the sidebar for a sample job ad.

Online Recruitment: Everybody's Doing It

Jobs ads you write for print publications can, of course, be repurposed to suit online posting requirements. Online recruiting has, in the last five years, eclipsed all other methods. A recent survey by Taleo, a manufacturer of on-demand talent management solutions, indicated that more than 80 percent of *Fortune* 500 companies post job openings on their corporate websites and nearly the same percentage have an online application process.

"The Internet has revolutionized recruiting and continues to change the way recruiters work," says Bryan Burdick, chief operating officer of ZoomInfo, a business information search engine. "Résumé databases give recruiters the ability to search large groups of résumés online, and social networks and search engines allow them to target candidates who may not be actively looking for a new position." Ginny Gomez, senior vice president of product management at Peopleclick, seconds that point. "New web-based contact relationship management applications allow recruiters to keep in touch with contacts before they are even looking for a job, letting them know as new positions become available that they may be a match for," she says. "These applications also facilitate reaching out to candidates who may have been a second or third choice for a position."

One of the most important but often-overlooked aspects of online recruiting is the corporate web presence. "Your company website is often the first contact candidates have with your company, so it must pique interest, provide comprehensive information on your company, and make it easy to search and apply for positions," says

Sample Job Advertisement

Financial Stock Administrator: Right Place, Right Time

Direct the successful administration of global stock option programs, employee stock purchase plans, and director equity plans at a time when XYZ's cutting-edge information retrieval technology has never been more in demand.

Your impact on our organization will be significant. From an accounting perspective, you'll play a key role in quarter-end financial preparation. From a communications standpoint, you'll ensure that all employees understand the value of the stock benefit plans that are a substantial part of their total compensation package. There will also be opportunities for you to stretch your skills by contributing to treasury activities such as cash management. Attendance at yearly NASPP conferences and monthly lunch meetings focused on professional development will further enhance your expertise and ensure your success in this career opportunity.

You'll leverage, ideally, a Certified Equity Professional (CEP) designation, plus deep skills in accounting and a strong aptitude with Equity Edge software to drive financial reporting of XYZ company's equity compensation plans. To hit the ground running, you'll need very strong Equity Edge, OptionsLink, and MS-Excel skills, including the ability to run macros and system imports and exports.

XYZ Company is a leading enterprise solutions provider helping organizations maximize the return on their investment in intellectual capital. This is a tremendous opportunity to join a stable, financially profitable company, while expanding the breadth of your skills into what normally are treasury-related functions.

Compensation starts at $65K and is commensurate with experience. To apply, please call (123) 555-5678 or visit xyzcompany.com.

This sample advertisement was provided by Martin Yate (2006), Hiring the Best.

Terry Laudal, senior vice president of human resources at SAP America. "Our e-recruiting software allows candidates to be masters of their own profiles, with the ability to modify their applications once they are logged in and fill out questionnaires and mini-assessments as well."

Other good features for career sections on corporate websites include the ability to forward information about a specific opening to another person, and email functionality that notifies interested applicants immediately when a suitable opening is posted. Many organizations also attempt to gain a competitive advantage by providing recruits with online features to make the job search process easier, such as résumé builders, company research tools, and industry advice articles.

Ginny Gomez also recommends the use of career microsites. "Would you reach out to a Baby Boomer for a C-level job the same way you would to a twenty-something applying for an entry-level position? Hopefully not," she says. "Instead, think about creating small portals for specific groups, targeting individuals by demographic, job type, location, campus, and so on."

Got the corporate online presence down? Then you no doubt also have experience posting openings on large, commercial job boards such as Monster.com, Hotjobs.com, and CareerBuilder.com. You may not, however, be familiar with one of the newest improvements in the online sourcing of candidates. In his article "Technology and the Hiring Process," James Ringler (2007), a research consultant with CorVirtus, says that many companies are now integrating requisition databases with corporate websites and external job boards. As a result, posting, renewal, or removal of job postings to the company website and external sites such as Monster.com occur automatically and in real time as changes occur in the requisition database.

Commercial job boards also have prescreening features that allow you to more readily identify qualified candidates, which we'll discuss more in the next chapter. Still, to manage the influx of résumés you'll inevitably receive as a result of external postings, you should work with your information technology team to set up special, pre-routed mailboxes for them. Designate a different mailbox for each position, and assign members of your staff to monitor them on a daily basis. Such a process will prevent the flow of résumés from spiraling out of control.

If you really want to attract the right candidates, though, it's not enough to focus your efforts solely on your own website and on the larger boards. You must also target alternative online outlets such as alumni sites, federal and state department of labor sites, social and professional networking sites, technology user groups, and local communities. In particular, industry websites, which are smaller and more specialized and list specific types of jobs, are an excellent place to advertise appropriate openings. "Websites that are field-specific are a huge asset in finding great talent, and not necessarily talent just within the local market," says Kim Hahn, the founder and CEO of the multimedia company Intellectual Capital Productions. "Having a presence on these sites is much more effective than the old-fashioned method of posting a job ad in the newspaper." Use the worksheet in figure 2-1 on the next page to brainstorm keywords and phrases you can put into search engines such as Google and Yahoo! to uncover the most appropriate websites. A few examples include:

- engineering: National Society of Professional Engineers (nspe.org)
- entertainment: Broadcast Education Association (beaweb.org)
- financial services: American Financial Services Association (afsaonline.org)
- government: FedJobs (fedjobs.com)
- information technology: Dice (dice.com)
- nonprofit: Nonprofit Career Network (nonprofitcareer.com)
- publishing: Association of American Publishers (publishing.org)
- sales and marketing: Sales & Marketing Executives International (smei.org)
- science and research: ScienceCareers (sciencecareers.org).

College Recruitment: Staving Off the Brain Drain

Human resources circles are buzzing about the impending "brain drain" in American organizations—and with good reason. As we mentioned above, the Baby Boomers, the largest generation in our history, will begin retiring in huge numbers in the next five years, and because of slow population growth between 1966 and 1985, there aren't enough young workers to replace them. You, along with every hiring manager in every successful organization, will be competing for the best talent among the 7 million college graduates just joining the workforce.

The traditional college recruiting process is changing to meet the needs of the empowered, ambitious, and demanding Millennial Generation (see the Millennial Recruiting sidebar), and your relationships with this age group must begin while students are still in school. If you don't have a formal internship program under way, contact the career services offices at universities in your area to start one immediately. Because Millennials are eager to learn and supremely motivated to increase their skill sets, you don't necessarily have to pay interns a lot, but you do have to show them respect and offer them challenging and engaging work. For instance, IBM's Extreme Blue internship program makes sure that interns don't

Figure 2-1. Website Search Worksheet

Date _____

Prepared by _____

Position _____

Relevant Job Titles (e.g., database administrator, software engineer)

Relevant Geographic Locations (e.g., New York, California)

Relevant Fields or Industries (e.g., information technology, software development)

Relevant Organizations or Association (e.g., database management user groups, Information Technology Association of America)

Relevant Skills (e.g., database application development, quality assurance testing)

Relevant Tools (e.g., SQL server, Crystal Reports)

---

end up making photocopies; instead, they are paired with computer developers, doing real company work in global research labs. A strong internship program is a critical part of your entry-level recruiting strategy because it allows you to recruit and train the best talent before it is snapped up by competitors and also to observe individuals in action before making a substantial commitment to them.

In addition to interns, you should be targeting soon-to-be graduates. In the old days, college recruiting consisted of spending days at a time on the road, shepherding thousands of random students past a drab-colored booth. Now, however, successful college relations programs involve fully partnering with staff from campus career planning and placement offices. Christopher Pritchard (2007), author of

Millennial Recruiting

The Millennial Generation, born between 1977 and 1990, is technology savvy, socially conscious, and highly informed when it comes to their early career decisions. Here are tips for persuading these discerning twenty-somethings to choose your organization.

Put on your best face: "College students expect employers to be prepared," says Pattie Giordani (2005) in her article "Y Recruiting." "On campus, they expect to interact with skilled recruiters who can give specific information about opportunities and provide a realistic view of the organization's culture. Because of this generation's emphasis on personal contact, nothing is more important than the people an organization chooses to represent its face."

Show them how they'll fit in: "Millennials want to join an organization that reflects their own values," says Carol Kinsey Gorman (2006) in her article "Ready or Not, Here They Come." "That's why companies like Disney have applicants watch a video that explains their standards, rules, dress code, and expected behaviors before they even fill out an application." Millennials take jobs not because of money but because working for the organization will allow them to make a difference in the world—so show them how you can help them do that.

Use online tools: Millennials expect an intuitive and efficient company website and want to fill out applications and other basic information online. They also use the Internet to seek out the opinions and perspectives of their most trusted information sources.

"You have to seek out those sources and cater to the Millennials' near overreliance on technology," says David Hyatt, president of CorVirtus. "Ernst & Young, for instance, just became the first employer with its own page on Facebook, Sony created an internship recruitment video for YouTube, and Honeywell has a blog on its corporate website that human resources recruiting professionals use to communicate directly with prospective employees. Try to stay in tune with the popular criticisms of your company via the web and address those directly in your interviews."

One word of caution, though: Millennials don't want you to rely too much on technology during the recruitment process. Online interactions can be cold and dehumanizing, so remember to add personal touches wherever possible.

(continued on next page)

Millennial Recruiting (*continued*)

Connect them with someone their own age: Millennial candidates have been advertised to all their lives and as a result are somewhat cynical. Because they're most likely to trust each other, introduce them to a satisfied employee of the same generation who can answer questions and address concerns about the job.

Manage the relationship: "Candidate relationship management is a mindset that understands the importance of the relationship between the recruiter and the potential recruit," says Gorman. "The way a candidate is treated by recruiters sets the tone for his or her initial impression of the organization." These relationship management tactics include showing personal interest in each Millennial candidate, answering questions and providing requested information in a timely manner, and keeping candidates in the loop over the course of the process.

New technology applications that support ongoing tracking and communication are facilitating the relationship management of Millennial candidates. "Many recruiters are reaching out to potential candidates while they are still in their early years of college," says Ginny Gomez. "Candidate relationship management applications are a great way to keep in contact with the many Millennials you may be keeping your eye on for future work in your organization, particularly considering the upcoming labor shortage."

101 Strategies for Recruiting Success, recommends sending campus staff requisitions on a weekly basis, working with them to ensure that they have an adequate understanding of each position, and promising a personal phone or face-to-face interview for every qualified student applicant to whom they introduce you. When you're on campus, "meet with key faculty, staff, and student leadership," says Pritchard. "Ask them what organizations on campus you might contact, and if there are opportunities for you to present seminars or guest lectures."

Networking: Be Active and Visible

When you're a hiring manager, the importance of networking over the long term to be in constant contact with qualified candidates cannot be overstated. Ideally, you should become a member of at least one professional association pertaining to your industry. As a vice president at a top public relations firm, for example, I belonged to the Public Relations Society of America, the Word of Mouth Marketing Association, and the Chicago Interactive Marketing Association.

Membership in and of itself, however, isn't enough. To reap the recruitment benefits, you have to be active and visible in the organization—attending meetings, serving on committees, organizing learning opportunities, and volunteering for events. By mere virtue of your participation, you'll be introduced to local candidates in your field who may currently work for competitors and to well-connected executives who have a demonstrated commitment to the industry.

You can also take your affiliation a step further. Most professional associations have membership directories that are networking goldmines, and by proactively calling or emailing other members and introducing yourself, you can seek advice and perhaps direct referrals pertaining to your search. But first, make sure that you understand the organization's rules of engagement for discussing recruiting with members.

If association membership is something you enjoy, joining organizations that cater to managers and executives, special interests, and/or minority groups such as women, African Americans, Latinos, and professionals with disabilities might also serve you well. Even if you're not yourself a member of a minority, you can often apply for associate membership and use the opportunity to start a dialogue on the recruitment of diverse talent in your community.

Events: There's a Time and a Place

I'll start by admitting that I'm not a huge fan of job fairs, because neither I nor anyone else I know has ever gotten a position as a result of one. I think of job fairs as expo-like events involving the herding of human masses through look-alike booths staffed by low-level, bored human resources staffers who are just looking to add a hundred more names to their databases.

On the other hand, Martin Yate (2006), the author of *Hiring the Best*, believes that job fairs have their place, and that they are best suited to recruiting entry-level employees and to generate overall visibility for your organization. He recommends that before you rent a booth at a fair, you properly assess exactly what you're getting for your money. "The question is not whether any of the applicants you want will attend, but how many," he says. If you do decide to participate, "make sure your booth looks top-notch and that the people representing your firm are articulate, polished, and professional."

Open houses are another commonly used method for initiating face-to-face contact with a large number of potential recruits. In an open house, you invite candidates to an event at your organization's offices or a neutral offsite location, provide them with background on your company, and conduct initial conversations to determine interest and fit. Because open house events are expensive, you'll want to look at them in terms of their bottom-line results and how many qualified leads you can realistically expect. Here are a few additional open house tips:

- Determine the *purpose* of the event. For example, will informal cocktails that will serve as a sophisticated introduction to your organization suffice, or do you want to leave the event with a group of prescreened candidates in hand?
- Assess if it's appropriate to line up a *guest speaker*, such as an industry name or one of the organization's top executives. Such remarks can make an event more attractive to candidates.
- *Advertise* your event internally and externally, online and offline, and ask for RSVPs so you have some idea of the number of attendees.
- Resolve *security* issues for your visitors ahead of time, so you don't have problems admitting people to your building.
- Serve *refreshments* that suit the mood and time of day of the event, and print plenty of copies of your strongest *collateral* material.
- Recruit enough employees to *staff* the event, handling traffic flow and responding to questions.
- Execute a plan for *following up* promptly with all promising attendees.

The Mechanics of Third-Party Search Firms

Professional search firms are used frequently in all types of organizations, and they do have many advantages. Not only do they maintain healthy networks in their target industries, but they can also facilitate the hiring process by prescreening applicants so that you only interview the best candidates and by handling some of the finer points of negotiation.

The Harvard Business Essentials (2002) book *Hiring and Keeping the Best People* suggests that retaining a search firm makes the most sense for executive-level positions, when the candidate pool is large, and when diversification or a joint venture creates new job categories that your company lacks or does not understand. You should be careful *not* to use a search firm to source candidates who you could just as easily find yourself. I've heard more than one story of companies paying exorbitant placement fees to third-party firms, only to find out later that the same candidates had either applied directly to the company at some point or were listed in other channels already available to internal recruiters. If you do decide you need outside help, here are options to consider:

- *Contingency recruiting firms:* This type of agency is paid after a candidate is hired. It is responsible for candidate sourcing and initial recruiting, preliminary screening, and arranging interviews with hiring managers at the client company. The client company pays either a flat fee or a percentage of the first year's salary—typically 25 to 30 percent.
- *Retained or executive search firms:* Like contingency recruiting firms, these agencies are paid by the client company, not the job seeker. However, retained search firms are paid an upfront fee to perform a search. They receive an amount based on the first-year compensation package for the position, usually one-third on signing, one-third on the presentation of a short list of qualified candidates, and one-third on completion of the hire. The use of such firms is most appropriate for higher-level positions within an organization.

Companies that engage third-party search firms often have long-standing relationships with several agencies in one or both of the categories above. Before you sign a contract with a new firm, however, be sure to ask these questions:

- How long have you been in business?
- What are the professional qualifications of your consultants?
- Is your agency a member of the National Association of Personnel Services or the National Association of Executive Recruiters?

- May I speak with some current client references?
- Can I get information on your fees and processes in writing?
- So that I won't expect to see candidates from certain organizations, may I see a list of companies with which you have exclusive recruitment agreements?

Out-of-the-Box Sourcing Ideas

To give your recruitment program an extra boost, why not take the road less traveled? These little-known strategies might work wonders for you:

- Research and contact the social service and private nonprofit agencies in your area—many have employment programs that match disadvantaged candidates to jobs. Christopher Pritchard recommends organizations like the Lincoln Training Center in South El Monte, Calfornia (lincolntc.org).
- You might already be familiar with your state's Department of Labor, but did you know that many will assign you a dedicated staff member to search for registered workers that suit your position?
- Individuals coming out of the military and into the business world often make conscientious, loyal employees. Martin Yate suggests visiting the website of the Destiny Group (destinygrp.com) to recruit ex-military job seekers.
- If traditional third-party search firms don't meet your needs, you might consider the temporary-help option. Employing temps allows you to "try before you buy"—deciding if a potential employee is a good fit before paying all the costs associated with bringing him or her on full time. Just make sure you understand the conversion cost, or how much you'll have to pay the temp firm should you choose to hire the person.
- If you're looking for creative or technical types, devise a contest that will allow talented candidates to compete for the chance to win a job at your company. Form a partnership with your marketing department to promote the contest and turn it into a branding exercise for the company as a whole.
- Employee research firms are paid to do the dirty work of scoping out the best candidates currently working for your competitors. Pritchard mentions that a well-regarded firm of this type is WorkStream (workstreaminc.com), which locates appropriate individuals for your open requisitions and pre-screens them for you according to your exact specifications.

- Use Google AdWords or other web search engine paid marketing programs to buy combinations of key words or phrases for which your target candidate might be searching (for instance, you might purchase the phrase "engineering excellence" to attract top engineers looking to improve professionally).
- Layoffs are all too common in today's business world, and you can often find highly qualified candidates as a result of contacting the human resources professionals in affected neighbors and competitors, and working with them to hire displaced individuals into your organization.

The worksheet in Figure 2-2 will help you plan your overall sourcing strategy.

Figure 2-2. Sourcing Strategy Worksheet

Date _____

Prepared by _____

Position _____

Overall Budget _____

Internal Marketing

Intranet Posting Details:

Referral Program Details:

Print Advertising

Publication 1 Specs and Cost:

Publication 2 Specs and Cost:

Publication 3 Specs and Cost:

(continued on next page)

Figure 2-2. Sourcing Strategy Worksheet (continued)

Online Advertising

Job Board 1 Specs and Cost:

Job Board 2 Specs and Cost:

Job Board 3 Specs and Cost:

Website 1 Specs and Cost:

Website 2 Specs and Cost:

Website 3 Specs and Cost:

Events

Job Fair or Open House Details and Costs:

College Recruiting or Association Event Details and Costs:

Search Firms Retained

Firm 1 Specs and Cost:

Firm 2 Specs and Cost:

Firm 3 Specs and Cost:

Other Sources

Making It Happen

If you want to develop a well-rounded, versatile online recruiting program, it's not enough to focus your efforts solely on your own website and on large online job boards. You must also:

- Develop a systematized internal recruiting program that gives current employees opportunities to grow their careers and rewards them for putting forth qualified candidates.
- Target alternative online outlets such as alumni sites, Department of Labor sites, social and professional networking sites, and niche industry sites.
- Join professional associations pertaining to your industry and host well-conceived recruitment events.
- Determine the best use of professional search firms and employ them to facilitate the hiring process.

Narrow the Field of Applicants: Assess Where They've Been and Where They're Going

As a result of your combination of search strategies, you'll likely have no shortage of candidates to fill your pipeline. The question now is: How do you conduct prescreening so that you and your colleagues are only spending time reviewing the candidates that are the best fit for your organization? In this chapter, we'll discuss the automated, technology-based measures you can put in place to ensure the proper filtering of application materials. And once the right résumés have arrived in your queue, we'll address how to review them efficiently, and then how to conduct a time-saving initial phone interview with promising candidates.

Manage Your Flow with Applicant Tracking and Prescreening Software

A recent Aberdeen study indicated that companies that use e-recruiting software reduce the time it takes to fill an open position by between 53 and 60 percent. Human resources professionals are standing up and taking notice of these metrics, and web-based recruiting and screening tools have become the norm at the majority of organizations of a certain size. "Most large companies currently use this type of technology to help with the flow of applicants that comes in through their applicant tracking system," says Marlon Doles, senior human resources manager at Campbell Soup Company. "This is key for more specialized positions. It helps to weed out unqualified applicants that tend to post to many different jobs you may have available."

The most common type of automated recruiting technology is applicant tracking software, which provides a searchable database where recruiters can match candidates' skills with job requirements, reporting on candidate activity, and methods for communicating with candidates at all stages of the hiring process. Some applicant tracking software monitors job boards across the web and mines relevant résumés by using artificial intelligence to analyze word patterns in a résumé and determine if that person is a good fit for a particular job. Applicant tracking systems are often customized for a specific industry or are designed to handle special problems unique to an organization.

An applicant tracking system alone, however, does not involve any type of evaluation of candidates. That's where prescreening software—or tools that gather information or ask questions about a candidate's background to ascertain if that person meets minimum requirements—comes in. Rocket-Hire (Rocket-Hire.com), a recruiting software manufacturer that conducts an annual survey measuring web-based screening and assessment usage, claims that qualifications screening is currently the most common form of automated prescreen. Part of this trend, says Rocket-Hire, seems to be the relative simplicity with which basic job qualifications (such as education or years of experience) may be collected and evaluated.

Another advantage of automated prescreening tools is that selection criteria are applied consistently, unlike personal reviews of hard-copy résumés and employment applications, which can be quite subjective. As for developing your screens, David Hyatt, president of CorVirtus, cautions that, in most cases, taking your traditional application content and putting it online will not be sufficient. "The criteria developed for screening applicants should be based on minimum requirements. This is not the place to determine the best candidate but rather to determine who should not be considered further," says Hyatt. "The screen should be targeted, direct, and concise, thereby limiting the amount of time the applicant has to spend. Overall, the screen should ask the question, 'Does this candidate fit with the job role, position requirements, and our organization's culture?'"

Alice Snell, vice president of research at Taleo Corporation (taleo.com), a leading provider of on-demand talent management solutions, cites skills-based prescreening in particular as a good method for obtaining critical information about a candidate up front. Relevant questions or tasks based on your job analyses and descriptions may be incorporated into online job applications so that a candidate is automatically pre-assessed based on the skills and qualifications you require. An example of skills-based prescreening in action is a software company that runs a classified ad with a short piece of computer code, stating the function of the code and asking readers to improve upon it as part of the job application process. What's important about this type of prescreening, says Snell, is that the skill you're evaluating be directly applicable to job responsibilities and performance.

In 2007, the *New York Times* ran a piece about Google's innovation in the area of applicant prescreening. The search engine guru has created an automated way to search for talent among the more than 100,000 job applications it receives each month. Google's web-based recruiting mechanism asks job applicants to fill out an online survey that explores their attitudes, behavior, personality, and biographical details going back to high school. The questions range from the age when applicants first got excited about computers to whether they have ever tutored or ever established a nonprofit organization.

Google's tool uses an algorithm that identifies candidates who resemble existing top performers in the organization and evaluates a much wider range of potential success predictors than typical methods of assessment, which tend to overemphasize academic performance, test scores, and subjective interview results. The tool calculates a score from 0 to 100, which allegedly predicts how well a person will fit into Google's chaotic and competitive culture. As of this writing, it's too early to tell how well the system is working for Google, but one can only imagine that it saves the company a great deal of time and money by screening out candidates who are blatantly poor matches.

Several of the large job boards have jumped on the prescreening bandwagon. Career Builder's subscription-based tool, for example, has a "My Screeners" page that allows you to ask 20 weighted questions and evaluate and score candidates accordingly. For each application, a percentage score representing the candidate's compatibility with your screening questions appears alongside his or her résumé. When it comes to standalone solutions, integration with applicant tracking systems is a trend that's quickly catching on among hiring organizations. For instance, software such as Success Factors' Performance and Talent Management module manages job requisitions, creates prescreening questions using a fully configurable Question Library, delivers job postings to internal and external websites, supports applicant tracking workflow, and reports on Equal Employment Opportunity Commission compliance, job requisition status, and candidate source metrics.

In addition to considering the legal issues that automated prescreening calls into play (see the sidebar), you must think about what this type of tool tells potential new hires about your organization. "Too many systems work in a spirit of exclusion, assuming there are more people out there than jobs," says Michael Sproul, founder of eBullpen, an online talent network. "A lot of damage is done to the company brand when people are not treated with respect. I know somebody who applied for a job at a firm on a Saturday afternoon and was rejected at 5 a.m. the following day. Nobody believes that anyone was examining applications then, and the experience left the person with a mild sense of outrage and a determination to flame the company any chance he gets." Adds Gerry Crispin, author of *Career XRoads:* "If you are comfortable enough to trust automation as a means to select in or out, then you need to be transparent enough in your deployment to share the results with the candidates themselves. Anything less will mean that your most qualified candidates might not participate, and you'll be left with a screening of B-level candidates at best."

Selecting the Software Solution That's Right for You

Investing in automated prescreening technology will likely serve you well as you seek to attract candidates whose traits complement your job analyses and descriptions, but with the hundreds of solutions out there, how do you choose the one that's right for you? Snell suggests that the most efficient approach involves framing the context of your needs and then gathering specific information (figure 3-1). You'll first want to establish solution objectives, such as improved quality of hire,

Legal Implications of Automated Prescreening

Hiring managers should be aware of the legal implications of using automated pre-screening. "Any procedure used to determine who will or will not move forward in the selection process is subject to antidiscrimination regulations," says Lisa Harpe, senior consultant with the Peopleclick Research Institute. "In addition, federal contractors are now obliged to comply with regulations specifically associated with Internet applicants. Federal contractors must solicit EEO information (like race and gender) on all applicants. Based on the definition of an Internet applicant, only job seekers who meet basic qualifications are Internet applicants. An automated pre-screening tool is extremely useful in identifying these job seekers, but the criteria should be based solely on basic qualifications that must be noncomparative, objective, and job related."

The information you collect from applicants via automated screening, is, in general, subject to scrutiny. Each state has its own hiring requirements, and you must make sure that you are aware of the laws both in the state you're in and in the states you're recruiting people from. "California laws place a lot more limitations on the amount of information employers can collect than might be the case in Texas," says Gillian Flynn (2002) in an article published in *Workforce Management*. "So if you're collecting information from someone in California, and you're based in Texas, but you're doing it all electronically, whose law governs? Could you be collecting information from that California person that would be lawful if you were both in Texas, but may not be in California?"

You also must be vigilant that your screening tool doesn't filter out groups of people from various protected categories. Flynn tells of a lawsuit against Walt Disney World, alleging that their prescreening software created a sort of reverse selection process. Rather than deleting résumés, the tool picked out the ones that had the words or phrases the company was looking for. The argument was that the words used by the software were not necessarily the same words that members of the African American community would use to convey information. They might very well be qualified for that job, but they didn't use the same terms that the software was using, because those were terms that would primarily be used by Caucasians.

The bottom line is that before you use automated prescreening technology, you need to get assistance and input from your legal counsel to ensure that its implementation helps rather than hinders your hiring efforts.

streamlined workflow, reduced time-to-hire, global process integration, and improved efficiencies. Next, you'll need to consider the type of staffing the chosen solution will cover (professional hires, hourly hires, internal redeployments, campus recruiting, contingent and contract workers, and the like). Finally, you should discuss the implementation with other stakeholders and come to an agreement as to whether you'll introduce the new solution in phases, via a pilot in one location, or via a simultaneous rollout across multiple locations, divisions, or business units.

Once you've gathered this information, says Snell, your software selection team should develop a short list of market leaders and work to uncover answers regarding the following categories of information (additional information regarding vendor selection is available at Taleo.com):

Vendor profile:

- What is the track record of each vendor? Does each have quality references?
- Is the vendor financially stable; will it be in business for ongoing support, maintenance, and upgrades?
- Who is on the management team?

Functionality:

- Is the software designed for professional hires, hourly hires, internal redeployment, campus recruiting, and contingent and contract workers?
- Does a demo of the software and features align with your current or preferred business processes?
- Is the solution scalable for future expansion?
- Does it support global processes, if applicable?
- Does it provide reporting, benchmarks, and metrics?

Implementation:

- What is the implementation methodology and timeline?
- Does the vendor have a history of on-time, on-budget implementation?
- What are the arrangements for training?

Support:

- Is support provided onsite, online, or by phone?
- When is support available? 24 × 7 × 365?
- What languages is support provided in?

Figure 3-1. Project Scope Worksheet

Date _____

Prepared by _____

Project Objectives

Solution Environment

Number of exempt employees covered by this solution: _____

Number of nonexempt employees covered by this solution:_____

Number of locations: _____

Supported languages:_____

Number of recruiters who will work with this solution: _____

Number of hiring managers who will work with this solution: _____

Number of expected new professional hires this year: _____

Number of expected new hourly hires this year: _____

Number of expected internal redeployments this year: _____

Number of contingent staffing suppliers: _____

Number of expected contingent assignments this year:_____

Current spending on contingent labor:_____

Rollout Plan

This worksheet was provided by Alice Snell at Taleo Research.

Information technology infrastructure:

- What technology does your company need to run this software?
- What programming languages and databases underlie the software?
- If the vendor is delivering an on-demand software-as-a-service solution, what is the expected uptime?
- What types of data security—such as encryption, virus scanning, or backup procedures—and physical security are in place?

Integration:

- Can the software be integrated with your organization's existing systems?
- What other companies have had integrations similar to what you will need?

Global expertise:

- Does the vendor have operations around the world?
- Can it accommodate several languages?
- Can it modify its processes according to the geography?
- Can it support all your locations around the world?

Reporting and metrics:

- What are the reporting and analytics capabilities?
- Does the vendor enable scorecards?

Pricing and return-on-investment:

- What are the costs? Are they all-inclusive?
- What are the maintenance and upgrades costs?
- Is there a proven case for return-on-investment?

After collecting all the data you can (figure 3-2), Snell recommends you cut your short list down to one or two finalist solutions based on the vendor's ability to meet business and technical requirements, as well as the vendor's service, support, and warranty; estimated investments; similar client installations; current client satisfaction; implementation plan; system performance; training capabilities; and contractual terms and conditions. The last step should be to design a service-level agreement that details the implementation and utilization of your new tool!

Figure 3-2. Vendor Selection Worksheet

Date _____

Prepared by _____

Name/Profile	Functionality	Implementation	Support	IT Specs	Integration	Expertise	Metrics	Pricing/ROI

Reading a Résumé: A Method to the Madness

Ideally, the use of an automated prescreening software solution will mean that the résumés that appear on your desk are already qualified in some way. But further evaluation is up to you, and your challenge begins with the first résumé scan.

Most people involved in hiring have read hundreds, maybe even thousands, of résumés. But is there any method to the madness? If you want to give every candidate a fair shot while getting through the pile quickly, there should be. To start, you should have your job analysis and job description in front of you when looking at a résumé that pertains to the open position in question. At the very least, you'll need to use these materials to ascertain whether the applicant has the requisite education, experience, and hard skills to warrant further consideration. When assessing education, remember the point from chapter 1 that credentials may be exaggerated or even fabricated. "You should recognize, though, that over time, professional experience gradually replaces educational attainment in degree of importance," says Martin Yate (2006) in his book *Hiring the Best*.

Now, you'll want to look for a pattern of achievement and results. After all, you want to know if a candidate has a history of making tangible contributions to his or her employer. But there's a caveat here, too. "Your task is to separate the fact from the fiction," says Yate. "Achievement claims relate to productivity—earning money, saving money, and saving time—and you should spotlight any that seem implausible and warrant further examination." For example, a software developer might say that his new human resources application allowed his former company to prescreen potential employees 25 percent faster. When presented with a claim like this, you will want to ask where that percentage came from. How were metrics of success documented? Also, what was this employee's role in building this particular application? Did he design and deploy it from soup to nuts, or was his job limited to one part of the execution? Take notes so that you remember to follow up on them later.

Along with results, you'll want to determine if the candidate's career trajectory makes sense. Did she move up the ladder in a predictable manner, commensurate with her achievements? If the résumé doesn't list starting and ending dates for the jobs listed (including the month and the year), you'll want to find those out in your phone interview. Learning starting and leaving titles—and salaries—is obviously useful as well. A pattern of short-term employment or repeated lateral moves may signal trouble. Candidates will probably try to spin—or leave off altogether—unflattering information. Your job is to read between the lines.

Last but not least, you should look carefully at the format and presentation of the document. Though the one-page rule has generally now fallen out of favor, résumés of any length should still be neat, well-written, and free of any typos or spelling errors. Managers searching for a candidate in an artistic position might pay more attention to graphics and layout, while information technology professionals should be on the lookout for concise explanations regarding how specific technical skills mapped to business objectives.

If you've decided not to pursue a candidate based on his or her résumé, make sure it's for the right reasons. Be careful of unconscious biases you might be carrying—for example, the person is not the typical age for the position, doesn't live in a good neighborhood, or got an undergraduate degree from your school's archrival. These things are simply not important compared with the candidate's inherent ability to do the job.

Telephone Interviews: 15 Minutes Now Will Save Hours Later

The phone screening interview is typically overlooked because hiring managers want to move straight to the in-person interview. However, you can learn a lot from a 15-minute phone call, enough perhaps to save yourself the trouble of entertaining an unsuitable applicant for an hour or two at your office.

The purpose of a phone screening is to determine if a candidate has the basic qualifications so that you can make an educated decision regarding an in-person interview. Once you've set aside résumés that show potential, arrange for a quick call to meet each candidate. You don't necessarily have to make all these calls yourself. Employees on your staff can be trained to conduct phone screenings for applicants at their level or below.

Your first questions in a phone screening should address any critical questions you have as a result of reviewing the candidate's résumé. If you've circled a potential deal breaker, you'll want to get clarification on it before bringing that person into the

Innovex Case Study

The pharmaceutical industry has experienced several major changes in recent years. An increased number of blockbuster drugs, a reduced product pipeline, and patients increasingly having limited access to physicians have all changed the way that drugs are marketed and sold. New pharmaceutical sales representatives need to be able to adapt to the changing aspects of this industry while also successfully promoting their products.

A pharmaceutical company needed to hire a new sales team of 235 representatives to sell a newly developed high-potential drug. The company decided to outsource the building of its sales organization, choosing Innovex. Innovex's hiring system was somewhat structured, but its field managers were heavily involved in time-consuming activities. Thus, the quality of candidates was inconsistent, and the system's cost per hire varied based on hard-to-fill territories. Innovex needed an efficient method of finding the very best sales representatives within a short period.

During the past eight years, Innovex has built more than 110 salesforces in the United States, comprising more than 14,000 hires. With more than 20 years in the global health care marketplace, the organization has been a partner of choice within the pharmaceutical industry for providing flexible, high-quality, and innovative sales and marketing solutions designed to accelerate the success of pharmaceutical, biotechnology, and other health care clients' products. A key service area for Innovex is supporting and managing the hiring of both permanent and contract sales professionals.

Innovex partnered with Development Dimensions International to implement Web-Screen, an online system to attract and screen applicants for sales representative positions. The new selection system included a broad range of measures designed to fully assess candidates in these areas:

- Who I am: dispositions and work styles
- What I have done: work experience
- What I can do: competencies and technical skills
- What motivates me: motivational fit.

Based on this assessment, candidates were classified into "bands," indicating their priority for being passed on to the next selection phase. The bands were calibrated to Innovex's criteria for job success in the sales representative role.

Innovex integrated Web-Screen with other assessment tools, and in the nine months following the hiring of the salespeople, the difference in their performance was obvious. The new hires were outperforming current employees in market share and total product prescriptions. The difference in market share between the two groups represents a significant dollar amount, exceeding $2 million. Overall system effectiveness has increased significantly compared to the previous system. Field managers are much more satisfied and feel that the system produces higher-quality new hires. These new hires typically have a shorter learning curve and show real strengths in overall performance.

This case study was provided by Development Dimensions International. Copyright 2004 by Development Dimensions International, Inc. All rights reserved. Reprinted with permission from Development Dimensions International, Inc., and Innovex.

office. Here are a few additional conversation ideas from Yate for getting a top-line, well-rounded view of the candidate in a short period of time:

- *Track record:* Of all of the work she has done, where has the applicant been the most successful? Look for answers that demonstrate her ability to contribute in your most crucial areas.
- *Current job:* How does his current job relate to the overall goals of his department or company? This response should demonstrate that the candidate understands how his efforts fit into the big picture. If the candidate is currently unemployed, his answer can reflect his last full-time position.
- *Preferences:* What aspects of her job or company does the candidate like best, or what would she change? This answer will help you determine if she will enjoy and will be successful working within your culture.
- *Future direction:* What is the applicant looking for in his next job? Look for a match between the candidate's needs and what your opening can genuinely provide.

Are you satisfied with the answers you received? Then it's time to bring the candidate in. Let's move on to the mechanics of preparing for and conducting a useful in-person interview.

Making It Happen

Web-based recruiting and screening tools have become the norm at most medium-sized to large organizations. Save your organization time and resources by

- installing applicant tracking software to keep track of candidate flow and match individual skills with position requirements
- selecting an e-recruiting software vendor with a prescreening tool that allows you to assess a candidate's background in the context of the position
- evaluating résumés by considering your job analysis and description and looking for a pattern of achievement and results
- conducting initial phone screenings to determine if a candidate is worthy of an office visit.

Create a Strategy for Interviewing: Make Every Minute in Your Office Count

---

In this chapter, you'll learn to

- avoid nondirected interview chitchat that tells you nothing of value
- structure the in-person interview so that you can objectively evaluate the candidate and sell your organization
- use behavior-based interview questions to assess prior work achievements
- get a real-world picture of your candidate with interview work simulations.

During the past few decades, much research has been done on the effectiveness of employment interviews. Most evidence resulting from these studies has demonstrated that interviews have low reliability and validity, yet everyone continues to rely on them as the principal way of determining the future of their organization. There are many reasons why in-person interviews don't work particularly well, the simplest of which is that people don't know how to do them. I'll admit that before I started researching this book, I treated all my interviews as casual conversations. Until now, you may have taken that approach as well. I hope that the information in this chapter will ensure that all the work you've done up to this point—from your job analysis to your upfront screening—was not done in vain.

Do Your Preparation in Advance

As you'll see, doing an in-person interview correctly is a relatively time-consuming process, so you'll want to make certain that you're only inviting in the strongest prospects based on your initial résumé screenings and telephone interviews. If you can swing it, schedule all your in-person interviews for a single position during the same week. Take the time to review each résumé again so that you can recall your initial questions and generate new ones. Though it's appropriate to tailor some of your inquiries to each candidate, it will be easier to compare apples to apples if you develop a core set of questions that all interviewees are required to answer. A standardized set of questions will also protect you in the eyes of the law. "Many employers forget or would like to forget that an interview is a selection procedure and, therefore, subject to antidiscrimination regulations," says Lisa Harpe, senior consultant with the Peopleclick Research Institute. "The interview should be structured with questions to ask every candidate and scoring that objectively evaluates each response."

Create at least two questions for each of the criteria identified in your job analysis and description (figure 4-1). Each question should also have a rating scale attached to it. For example, you might determine that an answer will be rated from 1 to 5 (with 1 being poor and 5 being superior), providing a description of what encompasses a "superior" response and a "poor" response.

What are the best types of questions to ask? Several full-length books have been devoted to this subject, but I'll share some guidelines from Martin Yate (2006), author of *Hiring the Best*:

- *Adaptability and suitability questions:* These show the candidate's skill set and test his understanding of the problems that must be solved, the problems he is there to avoid, and what he's there to produce. *Examples:* What would you say were the most important responsibilities in your previous job? What was the most difficult project you tackled in your previous job? With all your responsibilities, how have you planned and organized your workload?

Figure 4-1. Standard Interview Question Worksheet

Date _____

Prepared by _____

Open Position Job Title_____

Education

Selection Criterion 1 _____

Question A _____

Rating Scale A _____

Question B _____

Rating Scale B _____

Selection Criterion 2 _____

Question C _____

Rating Scale C _____

Question D _____

Rating Scale D _____

Experience

Selection Criterion 3 _____

Question E _____

Rating Scale E _____

Question F _____

Rating Scale F _____

Selection Criterion 4 _____

Question G _____

Rating Scale G_____

Question H _____

Rating Scale H_____

(continued on next page)

Figure 4-1. Standard Interview Question Worksheet (continued)

Skills

Selection Criterion 5 _____

Question I _____

Rating Scale I _____

Question J _____

Rating Scale J _____

Selection Criterion 6 _____

Question K _____

Rating Scale K _____

Question L _____

Rating Scale L _____

Personality Traits/Management Style

Selection Criterion 7 _____

Question M _____

Rating Scale M _____

Question N _____

Rating Scale N _____

Selection Criterion 8 _____

Question O _____

Rating Scale O _____

Question P _____

Rating Scale P _____

- *Motivation questions:* These demonstrate whether the candidate will be someone who comes to work with the intention of making a contribution and wants to spend the day engaged in focused activity. *Examples:* What personal qualities do you think are necessary to make a success of this job? What have you done that you are proud of? Think of a crisis situation in which things got out of control. Why did it happen, and what was your role in the events and their resolution?

- *Teamwork and manageability questions:* These showcase whether the candidate will be a cohesive influence, and whether her work style will mesh with your management style. *Examples:* Describe the best manager you ever had. In what areas could your last boss have done a better job? Tell me about an occasion when there were objections to your ideas. What did you do to convince others of your point of view?

- *Management questions:* These illustrate that the candidate will be successful at hiring and training, as well as getting work done through others. *Examples:* How do you quantify your results as a manager? Tell me about an occasion when, in difficult circumstances, you pulled the team together. What are the common reasons for resignations in your area of responsibility?

- *Entry-level questions:* These test a candidate's potential ability to do the job when she has little or no prior work experience. *Examples:* How did you spend your vacations while at school? What have you done that shows initiative and willingness to work? What job in the company do you want to work toward?

Richard Chang, CEO of performance improvement consulting firm Richard Chang Associates, also recommends that you ask questions that get to the heart of an individual's passion. "Look for people who have demonstrated that they have pursued experiences they were passionate about as they have matured—particularly with their own professional development," says Chang. "Have they made career and life choices based on what is in their heart versus making choices based on their head or what others have told them to do? Were they excited about how they applied their passions in previous roles? Recognizing the critical importance of shared passion in employees, Southwest Airlines CEO Herb Kelleher has been quoted as saying: 'We can teach the job—we can't teach the attitude.'"

It's a good idea for multiple people on your team to evaluate each candidate. The organizational psychologist Ben Dattner suggests that you look for interviewers with the following attributes:

- knowledgeable about the role, the team, and the organization
- representative of diverse groups within the organization
- reluctant to jump to conclusions
- open-minded and able to revise opinions
- self-aware and able to account for their own biases
- accurate in their predictions of candidate success over time.

The group should be coordinated on the roles that each interviewer should play. "If a candidate is interviewing with four people, each person should be designated specific questions so that all four people aren't asking the same things," says Terry Laudel, senior vice president of human resources at SAP.

Because your prospects will receive their first impression of your organization before they even sit down with you, make sure that there are processes in place to make interviewees feel at home immediately. Access to your building or floor should be hassle-free, and candidates should be provided with friendly reception and a pleasant waiting environment. Provided your interviewee isn't extremely early, send someone down promptly to escort him or her to the interview location—or better yet, go yourself. And try to do the interview in a conference room or private lounge so that you can avoid tempting distractions and the appearance of being on "your turf."

The Dance of the In-Person Interview

According to the Harvard Business Essentials' (2002) book *Hiring and Keeping the Best People*, the opening of the interview should take about 10 percent of the allotted time, and your goal is to make the candidate feel sufficiently comfortable to open up and to set expectations for the conversation ahead. The bulk of the interview, or approximately 80 percent of the time, should be used to gather the information you'll need to objectively evaluate the candidate and sell your organization. The final 10 percent of the time is your wrap-up.

Once you've finished chitchatting and it's time to get down to business, tell the candidate you plan to take notes. At this point, begin your line of questioning in a chronological order. "Starting with education, you need to understand the candidate's course of learning and the reason for choosing that field of study," says Steve Springer (2006) in his book *Stop Hiring Failures*. "This approach also allows you to evaluate the person's career in a logical order." In addition to the scripted items you've prepared, these types of questions from Yate might come in handy as you proceed through the meeting:

- *Closed-ended questions:* These mandate a yes-or-no answer and are useful for getting commitment or refreshing your memory. *Example:* Can you start on Monday?
- *Open-ended questions:* These demand an explanation in response and keep the candidate talking. *Example:* How do you respond to that kind of pressure?
- *Negative balance questions:* These probe for the negative when a statement seems too good to be true. *Example:* That's very impressive. Was there ever an occasion where things didn't work out so well?
- *Reflexive questions:* These help you maintain control of the conversation and proceed with other topics. *Example:* With time so short, I think it would be valuable to move on, don't you?
- *Hamburger helper questions:* These make the answer go a little further when you need more information. *Example:* You said that you worked with marketing to increase annual unit sales by 25 percent over 12 months. What was the nature of your contribution? How were sales increased, by more effective selling or by slashing prices?
- *Mirror statements and silence:* These paraphrase a key statement from the answer, followed by interested silence. *Example:* So, whenever you are two hours late for work, do you stay late for two hours to make up for it?

Throughout the course of the discussion, talk openly and enthusiastically about your organization's successes, what makes it different, and the variety of opportunities that would be available to the applicant. But don't fall prey to one of the most common mistakes interviewers make: telling the candidate directly what you're looking for. "Avoid providing the candidate with any information that reveals your requirements for the position, because the applicant will attempt to present his or her background in the best possible light," says Springer. "If you provide any negative feedback, most candidates will quickly reverse their responses. Your job is to obtain as much information as possible, including any evidence that indicates a poor match to your requirements."

If you're new to the process of interviewing or have been working in another country, you should also know that there are certain things that are illegal to ask. Prohibited questions in the United States include:

- How old are you?
- Are you married?
- What is your citizenship?
- What is your sexual orientation?
- Are you disabled?
- What year did you graduate from high school?
- Do you have children?
- Have you ever been arrested?

Ask your legal counsel or human resources representative for a complete list of prohibited questions to ensure that you're staying on the right side of the law.

Your interview wrap-up should include asking for contact information for at least two references. Ideally, these should be former managers, but if this isn't practical they should at least be people the candidate has worked with fairly recently. If you are not working with a recruiter who has the responsibility of discussing compensation with the candidate, now is also a good time to bring it up. Your goal should be to get the candidate to tell you specifics regarding what he or she is looking for with respect to base salary, bonuses, and other benefits or perks. "The candidate's requirements should be near her present compensation, but you should never reject an applicant because the requirements are a bit beyond what you wanted to pay," says Springer. "It's possible that you'll find that your pay package is not consistent for the market for that level of person."

Make sure that you allow at least a few minutes for the candidate to ask questions, which you should, of course, answer honestly. If there are any undesirables associated with the open position, it's best to disclose them now, before either you or the candidate is too invested. If your colleagues have already interviewed the candidate or won't be doing so today, you should explain the remainder of the process before escorting the applicant out. Provide dates and times for a second interview or final decision, leaving plenty of wiggle room for the inevitable delays.

Once you escort the interviewee out, organize your notes for easy reference later on (figure 4-2). Evaluate the candidate's responses against the rating scale for each of your scripted questions. "Be sure to use the rating scale as your standard as opposed to comparing one candidate to another," says David Hyatt, president of CorVirtus. "Doing so may lower or raise your standard, making the interview process inconsistent from one person to the next."

After all your first meetings have been completed, you'll want to meet with your fellow interviewers to discuss the ratings for each candidate. Unfortunately, it's not unusual for different interviewers to disagree on some aspect of a particular person. This is one of the reasons a second interview based on an actual work task can be helpful.

The Second Interview: Work Simulation

In many instances, a second interview may be needed to more completely assess whether a particular candidate is well suited to your open position. Work simulations, sometimes also known as case interviews, provide candidates with a real-life business problem similar to one that might be faced on the job.

Steve Springer recommends that you use real rather than fictional problems for work simulations, because real problems are always more complicated and difficult than anything you could make up. For instance, if you are evaluating a marketing manager's strategic thinking ability, perhaps you could have a candidate develop a potential launch plan for a product you rolled out last year. On the other hand, if you need to test whether a bank administrator knows how to use your accounting software, you could ask the candidate to complete an assignment using that tool. If the position you're hiring for isn't your own, it's smart to enlist the help of people currently doing the job in question so you can put together the most appropriate simulation.

Although you should certainly be interested in the solution the candidate derives for your simulated problem, you should also pay attention to the process by which he arrived there. Did he ask for a suitable amount of background information? Were his questions pertinent and thoughtful? Did he proceed through the right channels and call on the appropriate resources? If relevant, did he develop a realistic timeline and budget? Figure out how you will evaluate success on the simulation in advance (for example, a rating scale from 1 to 5 on certain attributes or a checklist of completed steps).

Figure 4-2. Interview Assessment Form

Date _____

Prepared by _____

Open Position Job Title _____

Candidate Name _____

Contact Information _____

Education

Question A Notes

Rating _____

Question B Notes

Rating _____

Question C Notes

Rating _____

Question D Notes

Rating _____

Experience

Question E Notes

Rating _____

Question F Notes

Rating _____

Question G Notes

Rating _____

Question H Notes

Rating _____

Skills

Question I Notes

Rating _____

Question J Notes

Rating _____

Question K Notes

Rating _____

Question L Notes

Rating _____

Personality Traits/Management Style

Question M Notes

Rating _____

Question N Notes

Rating _____

Question O Notes

Rating _____

Question P Notes

Rating _____

Personal Interests and Professional Affiliations

Potential Issues

Requested Compensation

References

Follow-up

Some companies are taking work simulations a step further and engage in trial employment with candidates before bringing them on board permanently. "I think that before hiring someone, it's best to test them out on a specific project or proposal," says Kim Hahn, founder and CEO of the multimedia company Intellectual Capital Productions. "When we searched for one of our most senior positions, we brought a person on as a consultant for a two-month strategic project, which gave us the time to assess this person's capabilities, strengths, ability to deliver on what they said they could, and ability to fit within the culture of the corporation."

Work simulations are advantageous in that they showcase a variety of the competencies you're looking for and help candidates to understand exactly what the job entails. However, they do take much more time and effort on behalf of the hiring manager, so you'll want to make sure you reserve this type of interview for candidates under serious consideration.

Interviewing Dos and Don'ts

In addition to what we've discussed already, here are some tips for getting the most out of each in-person interview:

- *Do* look for candidates who are different from you and will add variety to your team. Recognize that human beings have the tendency to gravitate to people like themselves, but your goal should be to hire people who will complement your strengths, not duplicate them.
- *Don't* let first impressions get the better of you. Sometimes, you might meet a candidate whom you decide you want to hire immediately, and you might then ignore evidence brought forth in the interview that contradicts that opinion. This is known as the "halo effect."
- *Do* spend at least 45 minutes with every interviewee. Managers who think they can size someone up in 5 or 10 minutes are wrong, pure and simple. All the advance preparation in the world won't help you if you rush to judgment on a candidate.
- *Don't* put too much stock in "name brands." Just because a candidate went to a top school or is currently with a prestigious firm doesn't mean he is right for your position.

- *Do* focus on the big picture. "Steel yourself against the seduction of star quality. Competence in one area can be mistaken for or can masquerade as competence in another area," says Francie Dalton of Dalton Alliances. A candidate might be amazing in one area, but if her skill set isn't a good match for the whole job as defined in your job analysis, you should probably keep looking.

- *Don't* write someone off just because he's quiet or unruffled. What comes across as a low level of enthusiasm or a lack of motivation may just be his interview persona, and he could in fact be quite competent and able to do the job superbly well.

- *Do* move on to a new question if you see that a candidate is visibly uncomfortable. The candidate may be nervous, so give her the benefit of the doubt. Once things are back on track, you can either rephrase it or ask for the same information in a different way.

- *Don't* let a candidate take over the meeting with his own agenda. If he's talking too much and time is sliding by, politely interrupt by saying: "I'd love to hear more about that, but for now may I ask you about … ?"

- *Do* look for red flags that could indicate a potential problem and probe for explanations. Dora Vell of Vell & Associates gives an example: "Be on the alert for blushing, sudden loss of eye contact, sudden twitching, stammering, or fidgeting, a significant change in the pace of speaking, heavy perspiring, or inconsistency between nonverbal behavior and words."

- *Don't* think you can change a candidate. Her prickly personality has gotten her this far and she's not likely to bend now.

- *Do* assess the likelihood of retention. It costs a lot of time and money to hire someone, so you want to be sure he's going to stick around a while.

- *Don't* succumb to desperation hiring. When your organization is hemorrhaging and your employees are crying for mercy, you may feel great pressure to get someone in now. But shotgun hiring often results in fast turnover, and you don't want to find yourself in the same situation six months from now.

- *Do* look for patterns. Does a candidate have a history of making lateral moves? If so, you may be hiring someone who will want a different job in your company in a few months. Does she complain that all her previous companies were too bureaucratic? If that's the case, then she's likely to come to the same conclusion about yours.

- *Don't* tell your life story. The candidate is not there to hear about your career and experiences; he's there to tell you about his. Remember that when you're talking, you're not interviewing.

- *Do* permit the occasional pause. We all hate silence during a conversation, but resist the urge to jump in and help the candidate with her answer.

For an example of one company's interviewing strategy and process, see the Doc Chey's Asian Kitchen Case Study sidebar.

Doc Chey's Asian Kitchen Case Study

John Metz is a partner in the Georgia-based Doc Chey's Asian Kitchen, a restaurant offering fast-casual service during the day and full service at night. Last year, he worked with CorVirtus to develop a consistent interview process for hiring hourly and managerial workers. He says: "The new process allows us to learn much more about any potential employee way before they become a part of our team, and I think that's the biggest help."

Doc Chey's strategy is a process of elimination of sorts, creating standardized questions about what each restaurant operator needs in three categories: performance, fit, and retention. Performance addresses the candidate's skill and aptitude and whether or not he or she has the skills to do the job. The basics of the fit category include the hours of work a candidate is available, pay, and transportation. Also considered is the culture of the company. Will the candidate's personality and delivery provide the hospitality or customer service an operator needs? Retention questions might be: What's the candidate's job history? What's the likelihood of him or her sticking around?

Chelle Parks, director of operations and enterprise solutions for CorVirtus, says that homing in on these three characteristics is the best way to decide if a candidate is the strongest match for the position and your business. The questions should be behaviorally based on topics like team focus, operations awareness, service-mindedness, and hospitality. Answers are then scored and conclusions drawn.

CorVirtus emphasizes a standardized and structured system. "Structured interviews are absolutely the best way to go," Parks says. "There's so much research out there that shows that one structured interview is worth the time of three or four nonstructured interviews." Sample questions Parks might suggest to Doc Chey's or other restaurant industry clients include: "Why is it important for the front of the house and the back of the house to work well together?" "If a fellow team member isn't carrying their weight, what would you do?"

Parks maintains that these types of questions help the interviewer uncover whether or not the candidate understands the importance of certain concepts; they can also tell you a lot about a person's work ethic and attitude. "You can tap a couple of different areas with one question," she says.

Since implementing the new interviewing system, Doc Chey's has not lost a single employee.

This case study by Christa Gala was originally printed in QSR magazine in June 2006, and was provided to the author by CorVirtus.

Making It Happen

Your interviews should be strategic rather than casual conversations. Put yourself in a position to select the best candidates by taking these steps:

- Create a standard list of relevant questions and corresponding rating scales for each candidate.
- Schedule all interviews for a single position during the same timeframe, and structure each in a formal way.
- Talk openly about your organization's successes and differentiators, but avoid telling the candidate directly what you're looking for.
- Use behavior-based questioning and work simulations to further assess whether a candidate is a strong fit for the position (see the Behavior-Based Interviews sidebar).

Behavior-Based Interviews

A best practice interviewing technique is behavior-based questioning. Using this approach, the interviewer asks the candidate to talk about prior work achievements. The idea is that when a candidate gives strong and specific examples of past performance, interviewers can anticipate his or her future behavior on the job. "Asking candidates to provide descriptive examples of when they exhibited certain traits is an essential method for establishing candidate credibility," says Francie Dalton of Dalton Alliances. "The technique also helps interviewers subordinate their subjective 'gut feel' about a candidate to more objective criteria."

Steve Brittin of TWC Group, a recruitment and HR consultancy, offers the following scenario:

Company ABC is a midsized financial software company. The organization recently got approval to hire a software engineer. A job analysis was developed based on the incumbent, who had five years of C++ experience in an application development environment and a great deal of expertise developing financial software. The job analysis, however, did not mention that for the last year, the group had been struggling with performance and reliability of the software created by the incumbent. Additionally, the company was considering upgrading to the new version of Oracle.

Two candidates came in to interview. The first was from a large firm specializing in financial software. The other candidate was from a midsized telecommunications company. Both candidates had the same amount of experience developing applications with C++. On paper, it seemed like the first candidate was the better fit because he had developed similar financial products before. However, by using behavior-based interview questions, Company ABC determined that the first candidate had run into—and failed to overcome—the difficulties faced by the incumbent, whereas the second candidate had a track record of being one of the best performance engineers at her current firm and had also recently worked on a project with the latest version of Oracle.

Behavior-based interviews played a critical role in helping Company ABC decide that the second candidate's past accomplishments rendered her much more likely to succeed in achieving the objectives of the available software engineer position.

Do Effective Background Research: Verify Your Impressions with Supporting Data

In this chapter, you'll learn to

- make the most of reference checks by getting the person's perspective on the candidate's strengths and weaknesses
- conduct a background check that provides you with unfiltered information on the candidate's credentials, financials, and legal standing
- avoid the inherent biases of in-person interviewing and better predict on-the-job success with preemployment assessments
- implement a legally defensible drug-screening program.

You've gotten through the interview process, and you've identified a short list of candidates you believe would be excellent additions to your team. Congratulations, you're almost there. There's just one final step, and that's to do background research and any relevant assessments to make sure you have as much data as possible before presenting an offer. In this chapter, we'll discuss best practices for calling candidates' references, conducting background checks and credential verifications, and administering valid personality and skill assessments.

Making Reference Calls Count

By the time you've had your second interview with a candidate, you should have the contact information for at least two references in hand. Though you can email a reference initially, I highly recommend that you connect either in person or by phone with at least one reference for each candidate. Reference letters or emails can be helpful, but speaking with a person allows for a better interpretation of tone and for the ability to ask questions on the fly.

Some experts say that the primary goal of a reference call is to verify the basics of what the candidate told you in the interview, but I believe you need to do much more than that. After all, would a candidate really provide you with a reference who couldn't back him up on obvious things like how long he worked at a company and what he did there? What you should be looking for is the reference's perspective on the candidate's strengths and weaknesses as an employee. In this respect, you should ask open-ended questions about job accomplishments, intellectual ability, personality and character, interpersonal and technical skills, business judgment, level of commitment, management style, and areas for development. As in the interview, don't broadcast to the reference exactly what you're looking for.

The problem with most references is that they tend to be very vague in their comments. They don't know you from Adam, and so they don't want to say anything that might get them into trouble. John Uprichard, president of Find Great People International, suggests that you make the reference comfortable and more willing to offer honest and constructive criticism by using a less formal approach. "Try saying something like 'I'm calling to talk about your relationship with John. He gave me your name and mentioned you'd be able to tell me about some of his accomplishments and some areas in which he could improve,'" says Uprichard. "If you're still getting a pleasant but generic image of the candidate, rephrase your questions so that you're presenting the topic of a candidate's weaknesses in a nonaggressive manner. For instance: 'We are really excited about the possibility of bringing John on board. If he is selected for the position, what are some areas in which you think he could use some development?'"

If you're speaking to a reference and she mentions someone else you might want to talk to, take her up on it and get the person's contact information. Calling a candidate's references is not just an item to check off your list before making an offer. It's in your best interest to do everything you can to get to know the candidate as intimately as possible, and the more people you ask, the more complete your picture is likely to be.

You might also think about killing two birds with one stone. Calling references can be a good networking activity for you. Though the focus of the conversation should certainly be the candidate, it can't hurt to exchange information with other managers with respect to recruiting and business in general. You never know when you might meet someone who is in a position to help you again down the line. After you hang up the phone, organize your notes in the form of a reference report (figure 5-1) and send a note thanking the reference again for her time.

Don't Trust Everything You Read: Conducting Background Checks

A recent article in *Time* (Cullen 2006) suggested that many companies are hiring much less than they bargained for. One résumé-vetting company researched 1,000 résumés and found that 43 percent of them contained one or more "significant inaccuracies." As an expert in the *Time* article claimed, "There's a lot of evidence that those who cheat on job applications also cheat in school and life."

Even more disturbing is a study performed by CorVitus, which discovered that 17 percent of candidates being seriously considered by restaurant companies had been arrested one or more times, with 42 percent of that group having been convicted of the charge.

Because you can't necessarily trust everything you read on a candidate's résumé, and because unsavory aspects of an individual's past aren't likely to be disclosed in an interview, smart hiring nearly always involves some type of background check. Commonly addressed areas include education and employment credentials, credit history, and criminal and motor vehicle histories.

Education and employment credentials: As discussed above, many candidates embellish or lie outright about the amount and years of higher education attained. It's fairly inexpensive to verify this information through a source such as the National Student Clearinghouse or a website like DegreeCheck.com. Likewise, if you want to confirm that a candidate worked at a certain company or a certain period of

Figure 5-1. Reference Report

Date _____

Prepared by _____

Candidate Name _____

Position _____

Reference Name _____

Title _____

Company _____

Phone/Email _____

Years Known _____

Context _____

Undirected Impressions of Candidate

Examples of Major Accomplishments

Intellectual Ability

Personality/Character

Interpersonal Skills

Business Judgment

Technical Skills

Energy Level/Commitment

Leadership/Management Style

Areas for Development

Parts of this report were adapted from the Vell & Associates' Reference Report.

time and made a certain salary, you need not waste time calling a valuable reference. Verifying employment credentials merely involves placing a call to the candidate's old company's human resources department.

Credit history: A simple credit check can be performed through TransUnion, and, according to CorVirtus president David Hyatt, you should be looking for issues demonstrating that a candidate is irresponsible with money. "This can be seen as a reflection of how a candidate might handle the finances of the company to which they are applying," says Hyatt. "We look for things such as bankruptcies, collection accounts, repossession, and patterns of late payment history."

Criminal and motor vehicle histories: You can use your state's database to search criminal records, but some experts suggest that these tools tend to be unreliable. "Because many databases are only updated a few times a year, there's too great a chance that you'll pull outdated or inaccurate data," says Hyatt. "Instead, we send researchers to the county courthouse to retrieve criminal records personally." If the job in question includes driving a company vehicle, you might also want to do a motor vehicle records check to ensure that the candidate has a current license and is free of any driving-related convictions.

Like other issues of this sort, checking candidates' backgrounds requires that you comply with legal regulations such as the Fair Credit Reporting Act, so it may be in your best interest to use an experienced vendor. Background research companies include multinational conglomerates and small, regional firms, and you can usually select a variety of services based on your geographic location and the positions in question. Well-known vendors include AccuFacts (accufacts.com), Arrin Systems (arrin.net), Global Verification Services (global-verification.com), and Kroll Factual Data (krollfactualdata.com), but because you are trusting this company with such sensitive employee information, you should check references carefully before employing any firm.

Also make sure that your company of choice will provide the necessary supplemental information for all reports ordered. "Vendors should send you an Adverse Information Notice—a legal requirement—with each report, as well as a notes page that explains any strange laws that apply to the state or states where you are located," says Tom DeCotiis (2006) of CorVirtus.

If a background check procedure is a standard part of your hiring process, you or your recruiting staff should let candidates know about it upfront. "Because some candidates may have privacy concerns, inform them of exactly what will be expected—a drug test, a credit check, and so on—and tell them how long this information will be kept on file," says Lisa Harpe, senior consultant with the Peopleclick Research Institute. "In addition, you may want to disclose how this information will be used in the recruiting and selection process. If you don't explain this early on, be prepared to have this question asked at a later date."

Under certain circumstances, you may wish to obtain written permission from candidates to perform background checks. See figure 5-2 for a sample authorization form. The sidebar on page 72 gives information on drug screening, which can be another form of background check.

Getting Scientific: Preemployment Assessments

Rocket-Hire's recent online screening and assessment usage survey (Handler and Healy 2006) reported a significant increase in the number of organizations using scientifically based cognitive, skills, and personality tests. In 2006, 66 percent of surveyed companies used a skills assessment for employment purposes (up from 53 percent in 2005), and 65 percent used a personality assessment (up from 34 percent in 2005).

According to Rocket-Hire, the variation in the deployment of these types of tests and assessments is wide, with a total of 36 percent of survey respondents indicating that assessment is utilized in the placement of individuals into either all domestic (28 percent) or global (8 percent) jobs. These assessments are most commonly used for web-based managerial, sales, information technology, administrative, and customer service positions, in part because so many different instruments and recruiting programs have been developed specifically for these sorts of jobs. And their effectiveness? Sixty-three percent of assessment users felt their tools added value to their organizations.

Preemployment cognitive, skills, and personality assessments can be valuable additions to your arsenal of hiring tools. Not only do they assist you in finding the most appropriate candidate, they also help you avoid the inherent biases of in-person interviewing and better predict on-the-job success and whether a person will assimilate well into your organization. However, there are a few "rules of the road" you'll want to follow as you navigate this territory.

Figure 5-2. Background Check Authorization Form

Authorization for Background Investigation

Full Legal Name _____

If applicable, other names used during the last 5 years:

_____

Current Address: _____

Current Phone: _____

Current Email: _____

Social Security Number: _____

Date of Birth:_____

Gender: M / F

Position Applying for: _____

Residence History (last 5 years):

City and State	Dates Resided

As a candidate for the above-referenced position, I understand that [insert company name] may conduct a background investigation, including education and employment verification and credit and criminal record investigation, for employment purposes. If I am refused employment due to the results of the background investigation, I understand that I may request an explanatory meeting with [insert name]. Such a request must be made within 5 working days of my notice. Failure to provide complete and accurate information will be case for disqualification/termination of employment.

Signature: _____   Date: _____

Drug Testing

Preemployment drug testing is reasonably common, but employers often go about it badly. If you have good reason to open this can of worms, then you should be prepared to address questions regarding the rationale for obtaining such sensitive information, as well as how you'll ensure validity and protect employee confidentiality. Potential and current employees tend to be skeptical about drug testing, and their instinct is to distrust. Martin Yate (2006), author of *Hiring the Best*, suggests these steps for instituting a bulletproof testing program:

- *Work with a reputable firm:* Select a lab that has done work in your field for some time. Obtain strong references, and make sure the chosen tests are reliable. For more information, visit websites such as the Drug and Alcohol Testing Industry Association (datia.org), Drug Testing in the Workplace (corporatedrugtesting.com), and the Drug Testing Network (drugtestingnetwork.com).

- *Consult with your attorney:* Protect yourself from lawsuits by involving your legal counsel in the process upfront.

- *Establish strict guidelines:* Write clear policies for administering and processing tests and for protecting confidentiality of the results. Make sure the right personnel are in place to administer tests, and plan to do back-up procedures for all positive findings.

- *Share knowledge:* Talk with other employers about their successes and failures in setting up drug-testing programs.

- *Provide test takers with relevant information:* Give adequate notice, and alert test takers of the foods and medications that can lead to false positives.

First, assessments should be used as directed and in their entirety. "Let's say you go to the doctor and he writes you a prescription for an antibiotic," says Steve Brittin, a recruitment consultant with TWC Group. "The prescription says you need to take the medication twice a day for the full three weeks, but you think the drugs are too expensive so you only buy half of it and take it when you want. Would you really get better? Assessments work the same way." You should also make sure you use them consistently rather than selectively, meaning that all candidates who apply for the same job take the same test.

Second, preemployment tests are subject to antidiscrimination regulations, and the federal agencies responsible for implementing these regulations are increasingly interested in examining skills and personality assessments. "The Office of Federal Contract Compliance Programs routinely asks federal contractors about employment tests," says Lisa Harpe. "The Equal Employment Opportunity Commission has settled several cases in the last few years after claiming that various tests were discriminatory."

To be legally defensible, assessments must be designed for the hiring process, and all questions contained within them must have predictive validity, which means that they must accurately measure the traits they seek to measure and accurately predict behavior in the position in question. "An employer using or thinking of using an assessment should request evidence of the test's validity from the test vendor," says Harpe. "The test vendor should be able to supply this information, preferably in the form of a technical report. They should also conduct either a validity study specific to an organization to justify the test's use in that organization and for those jobs, or a transportability study to show that the jobs in question are sufficiently similar to jobs that have been included in other validity studies."

With respect to developing valid assessments, David Hyatt suggests these tips:

- Be sure that a representative sample is used to validate the assessment. All groups should be represented in validation studies to truly understand the real-world consequences of using the tools.
- Ensure that assessments are culturally sensitive. Some words convey different meanings within different cultures. Be sure to remove all language barriers and culturally insensitive content areas. Cultural differences can affect the validity of assessments in the hiring process. For example, some cultures (like China and Japan) emphasize group outcomes, but others tend to emphasize individual outcomes (like the United States and Europe).
- Personality is more closely related to the motivational aspects of work than to the technical aspects. Personality-based assessments are better for getting at what a person "will do" as opposed to what he or she "can do." Skills-based assessments are better suited to this latter purpose.
- Personality assessments are more predictive of performance in jobs where employees have a great amount of control as opposed to jobs where an employee has little or no control.

Helpful as assessments are, they aren't a magic bullet for identifying the perfect candidate. "Personality tests, skills assessments, and other tests are not, by themselves, decision tools," says Brittin. "They were never developed to be standalone products. Fortunately for us, there are still some human factors involved in the hiring process, and, yes, I am talking about a gut decision."

If you're thinking of rolling out preemployment cognitive, skills, and personality testing, you shouldn't attempt to go it alone. Talk with other human resources or hiring managers in other companies, or get advice from a third-party company or consulting psychologist specializing in these types of tests. Although outsourcing may require a significant upfront investment and a consulting psychologist can cost up to $2,000 per candidate, experts suggest that assessments are an aspect of hiring that you should do well—or not at all. If you take shortcuts, you could end up worse off than when you started.

Brittin tells this cautionary story: "A human resources manager designed some tests to assist in hiring for a new manufacturing facility. Because the company always pushed teamwork as part of the mission values, it seemed like teamwork would be a good thing to assess," he says. "So, he began interviewing for teamwork, created simulations that measured teamwork, and made hiring decisions based on teamwork. The result? There were 150 employees who would not hold a meeting unless everyone could attend, could not make a business decision unless everyone agreed, and wanted to regularly socialize after work. Meanwhile, the company had to implement an organizational adjustment to fix quality problems caused by people who would not confront co-workers producing poor-quality work."

Examples of Assessments

Do you need some preliminary guidance regarding the most popular cognitive, skills, and personality tests available? The organizational psychologist Ben Dattner generously provided the following overview.

Cognitive Assessments

Watson-Glaser Critical Thinking (harcourtassessment.com): The purpose of this assessment is to predict an employee's career path based on critical thinking skills. The attributes and abilities assessed include

- inference
- recognition of assumptions
- deduction
- interpretation
- evaluation of arguments.

Its logistics:

- 80 items
- approximately 60 minutes to complete.

Here's a sample item:

> Mr. Brown, who lives in the town of Salem, was brought before the Salem municipal court for the sixth time in the past month on a charge of keeping his pool hall open after 1 a.m. He again admitted his guilt and was fined the maximum, $500, as in each earlier instance.
>
> On some nights, it was to Mr. Brown's advantage to keep his pool hall open after 1 a.m., even at the risk of paying a $500 fine.
>
> True/Probably True/Insufficient Data/Probably False/False?
>
> Output: a score that is compared against norms.

Wonderlic Personnel Test (wonderlic.com): This assessment measures cognitive ability as an accurate predictor of employment success. The attributes and abilities assessed include a candidate's ability to

- solve problems
- learn a specific job
- understand instructions
- apply knowledge to new situations
- benefit from specific job training
- be satisfied with a particular job.

Its logistics:

- 50 items
- exactly 12 minutes to complete.

Here are sample items:

1. Two people caught 36 fish; X caught 8 times as many as Y. How many did Y catch?
2. Are the meanings of the following two sentences: (1) similar, (2) contradictory, (3) neither similar or contradictory? "It is always well to moor your ship with two anchors." "Don't put all your eggs in one basket."

Output: a score that is compared against norms.

Skills Assessment

Walden Sales Skills Test (Waldentesting.com): This assessment measures the knowledge, skills, and abilities required to succeed in sales positions. The attributes assessed include:

- knowledge of general sales principles
- knowledge of sales terms
- relevant vocabulary skills
- understanding of issues that can affect the sales process
- ability to deal with several sales situations
- basic mathematical and calculation skills
- logic and attention to detail.

Its logistics:

- 6 items
- exactly 65 minutes to complete.

Here's a sample item:

1. Below are seven key steps—a to g—in the selling cycle. They are in random order. On the lines provided, place the digits 1 to 7 to indicate the best logical order to execute these steps for a successful sale.

   a. addressing concerns
   b. presentation of the product
   c. getting referrals
   d. closing the sale
   e. prospecting
   f. qualification
   g. original contact

Output: candidate score and hiring recommendation. Example: "With an overall score of 81 percent, Ms. Logan strongly demonstrates the skills needed to succeed in a sales position."

Personality Assessments

16 Personality Factors (lpat.com): This assessment assists with selection by measuring five primary dimensions that frequently forecast management potential and style. The attributes and abilities assessed include

- warmth
- reasoning
- emotional stability
- dominance
- liveliness
- rule consciousness
- social boldness
- sensitivity
- vigilance
- abstractedness
- privateness
- apprehension
- openness to change
- self-reliance
- perfectionism
- tension.

Its logistics:

- 185 items
- approximately 35 to 50 minutes to complete.

Here are sample items:

1. I get new ideas about all sorts of things, too many to put into practice. True?/False?
2. I let little things upset me more than they should. True?/False?

Output: basic interpretive report. Examples: "At times, Mr. X may show the self-discipline and conscientiousness needed to meet his responsibilities. At other times, he may be less restrained, following his own wishes." "Typically, Mr. X tends to take things in stride and adapt to circumstances."

Guilford-Zimmerman Temperament Survey (pearsonassessments.com): This assessment measures attributes that may help predict successful performance in various occupations. The attributes and abilities assessed include

- personality traits
- temperament factors.

Its logistics:

- 300 items
- approximately 30 to 60 minutes to complete.

Here are sample items:

1. You give little thought to your failures after they are past. Yes?/No?
2. You like to sell things (that is, to act as a salesperson). Yes?/No?
3. You often crave excitement. Yes?/No?
4. You speak out in meetings to oppose those who you feel sure are wrong. Yes?/No?

Output: an interpretive report. Examples: "He usually avoids being surrounded by other people, and he tends not to initiate conversations with strangers." "He does not take things too seriously and is inclined to act impulsively."

Other tried-and-true tests recommended to me include the Personality Research Form (sigmaassessmentsystems.com), the Predictive Index (piworldwide.com; see the La-Z-Boy Case Study sidebar), and WorkKeys Skills Assessments (act.org).

La-Z-Boy Case Study

La-Z-Boy Inc. is an international retail furniture company with major distribution throughout North America. Corporate annual revenues exceed $2 billion. It uses the Predictive Index® (PI) system in its proprietary operation, which consists of stores in the Phoenix area with an employee roster of 200. The PI, developed more than 50 years ago, is an in-house management tool used by executives worldwide to place the right person in the right job and then harness each person's unique behavioral strengths for maximum productivity.

When Kathy Till joined the staff of the Phoenix La-Z-Boy network as director of training, she found that employee turnover was over 100 percent, a sure signpost of low job satisfaction and morale. She knew from experience the high toll employee turnover takes on a company's financial and psychological well-being. She also knew that La-Z-Boy would not achieve its goal of building long-term, repeat-buyer relationships without establishing a productive salesforce with a longer-term commitment.

Till made the decision to enlist the help of the PI and gave the PI survey to every employee. This enabled management to examine the behavioral patterns of all their employees and identify the profiles of their top performers. Using these behavioral traits as a model, management was able to supplement its salesforce with hires who matched the desirable gregarious, persuasive PI profile of the top salespeople. PI also enabled La-Z-Boy to identify the patterns of those employees who were underperforming in sales roles and to place a number of those individuals in positions better utilizing their natural abilities.

Over the next three years, the turnover rate was reduced by 30 to 40 percent in any given year. "By using the Predictive Index as an interview tool, I was able to hire the people whose personalities fit the requirements of the job and the needs of the company. Not only did we begin to hire smarter but also we made employees happier by better placing them in positions that matched their personality strengths and helped to ensure their personal success in the company," says Till.

This case study was provided by PI Worldwide.

Making It Happen

Before you present an offer, make sure you have as much objective data as possible. Don't forget to

- Check references by phone, and collect critical performance information through the use of open-ended questions.
- Undertake a background check that addresses education and employment credentials, credit history, and criminal and motor vehicle histories.
- Identify preemployment cognitive, skills, and personality assessments that will assist you in finding the most appropriate candidate for your organization.
- Seek assistance in selecting assessments that accurately measure your desired traits and predict future behavior.

6

Make the Job Offer: Expedite Your Decision and Finish Strong

A successful background check will, it is hoped, result in your decision to make an offer to your first-choice candidate; and either before or immediately after a verbal offer is presented, you should step up your efforts to sell the candidate on your organization. If the candidate is a very strategic hire, perhaps arrange a lunch or dinner so that she can get to know the individuals on your team personally. Anyone you're looking to bring onboard, however, should at least be invited back into the office for a brief meet-and-greet and a tour of the facilities. Candidates will feel better equipped to make a decision if they have a clear sense of the environment in which they'll be working and have the opportunity to get a feel for your culture by meeting the people they'll be working with each day.

This chapter addresses the mechanics behind making an official job offer, including the materials you'll want to send to showcase your organization, the advantages and disadvantages of using an employment contract, and managing the candidate's acceptance.

Don't Rush but Don't Dawdle: Making the Official Offer

As we've talked about throughout the course of this book, hiring is not a process that should be rushed. That said, however, you should do everything in your power to ensure that a decision is expedited and an offer is made to your top choice as soon as possible. Presumably, a strong candidate will have had multiple interviews and may even have several other offers in hand by the time you come calling. You don't want to lose the person to another organization simply because you didn't act quickly enough.

Just before you pull the trigger, you want to try to understand what the candidate is thinking. "Ask the candidate what would keep her from accepting an offer from the company, such as a counteroffer from her current company," says John Uprichard, president of Find Great People International. "Or, for example, if you're the human resources representative and you know that the position is a big change for the candidate and will involve a family decision, maybe ask if she wants her spouse to participate in a phone conversation with the hiring manager. These kinds of pre-offer questions will illuminate how the candidate really feels about the position."

Every organization has a different policy regarding who makes the job offer, a human resources representative or the hiring manager. Understand how the process works and don't attempt to buck the system. If it's your responsibility, make sure you speak to the candidate live, either in person or on the phone. I've read that the best time to make a job offer is Monday morning, because if you wait any longer, you risk not hearing back before the weekend.

Start by saying congratulations in a tone that makes the candidate feel special that he has been chosen. Provide an overview of the job again and what start date you're expecting. Ask the candidate if he has any questions or concerns, and, if you can, find out the names of the other organizations he is considering.

Unless you have a third-party negotiator (which some experts recommend), you'll also readdress the issue of compensation. By this time, you should have a good idea of what the candidate is looking for, and you want your numbers to fall within that range. Ideally, your organization will have an approved salary associated with each job title; but if not, you may need to do some research to make sure your offer is in line with industry averages and what the candidate is likely to receive from your competitors. An unappealing offer is likely to sour the candidate on your organization and the opportunity. (See the sidebar on salary decisions.)

In the end, however, if the candidate has asked for a higher salary than you or your company is prepared to give, propose your own number but be prepared to compromise on other valuable items such as bonuses, benefits, vacation allotment, stock purchase, and relocation. Depending on the candidate's level of seniority, you may need to educate her on the value of some of these "extras." For instance, though the salary you're offering might be a few thousand dollars lower, your extra week of vacation and superior health insurance plan could more than make up for it. If the individual will be eligible for a raise or promotion within a specific period of time, also mention that. Should any back-and-forth negotiation occur before a verbal acceptance, Dora Vell, CEO of Vell & Associates, recommends getting everything—complete offers and counteroffers—in writing.

Tell the candidate you're happy to give him 48 hours to think about the offer—and mean it. Deciding whether or not to accept a job is a huge proposition, and any decent candidate isn't going to be impulsive about it. Over the course of the next few days, provide the candidate with easy access to you in case he needs more information. Be prepared for the candidate to possibly come back and say that he would like to work for you but another company has made a better offer. If the candidate is top-notch, go a bit higher to match or exceed the competitor. Remember that when it comes to talent, you often get what you pay for.

While you're waiting to hear from your first choice, don't reject the other candidates waiting in the wings. It's not over until it's over, and you want to keep all your options open.

Assembling Your Offer Package

As soon as you've spoken with the candidate, you should send an offer in writing confirming the details of the hire. Your written communication should have the same tone as your conversation—warm and welcoming—and should include the

Deciding on a Salary

For many organizations, determining a set compensation package for each job title is a significant and time-intensive role of the human resources department. Assuming that you do not have this set package to work from, how might you go about deciding how much to offer a new hire? Here are a few tips to keep in mind:

- *Be competitive:* Use industry and local market comparison studies to make sure your compensation is in line with that of similar organizations with similar positions.

- *Align pay with your goals:* If you're charged with developing a highly skilled, outstanding workforce, you must pay above industry or regional averages to attract the quality employees you seek," says Susan Heathfield (2007c), the editor of About.com's Human Resources portal. "If, on the other hand, the strategy is to get cheap labor in the door quickly with little regard for turnover, you can pay people less salary."

- *Practice equality:* If you already have people working in the same function as the candidate, you should be offering a salary in line with what your existing employees are making. Taboo as it may be, issues of pay are often discussed in the workplace, and the last thing you want is for one of your best people to find out that the new hire came in earning $15,000 more.

- *Know the value of the whole package:* Benefits, especially health care insurance packages, have never been pricier, and how competitive your offerings are can and should affect the base salary you're willing to pay a candidate. You must understand how much it costs you to provide certain benefits to your employee and pass that knowledge on to the candidate during negotiations.

- *Don't use a poor economy as an excuse to pay less:* "You don't want to get too far out of line with what you would have paid that employee during better times," says Heathfield (2007c). "You risk losing her when the economy improves. She may never feel valued by your organization if her pay is out of line with her experience and contribution. She may never really stop her job search, using your company as a resting place until the right offer arrives."

proposed start date, job title and responsibilities, compensation, and decision deadline. It may also spell out certain conditions that must be met before you can officially hire the candidate, such as passing a medical exam, providing evidence of her eligibility to work in your country, and completing a successful probation period.

The sample job offer letter in figure 6-1 uses standard categories that cover most positions from production worker to director. As Susan Heathfield (2005) says, executive letters are often far more lengthy as the agreements reached can cover everything from compensation, moving expenses, and signing bonuses to millions of dollars in severance packages. Consult your attorney about any job offer more complicated or more extensive than this sample.

The offer letter should only be part of a more comprehensive package your organization sends to the candidate, a package that creates a memorable impression for your soon-to-be employee. Other items should provide information on the pay and benefits program, promotional literature, the in-house newsletter, product descriptions, and even an annual report. This type of information helps the candidate reconfirm his or her decision and can also be shared with interested friends and family.

You may also want to include a letter from the candidate's new supervisor. This might be nothing more than a simple handwritten note referring to something discussed during the interview or briefly outlining the department's achievements or objectives.

Even if the candidate has already accepted the terms of the offer verbally, you should still insist on a signed offer letter, and, if relevant, employment contract, confidentiality agreement, and noncompete agreement (see figures 6-2 and 6-3).

The Employment Contract: To Use or Not to Use

An employment contract puts forth the terms of the relationship between you and the candidate moving forward. Its purpose is to delineate the job the candidate is being hired to do, and what he or she can expect to receive from you—the employer—in return. Sometimes, written employment contracts also include the length of the assignment, grounds for termination, and policies for intellectual property created on company time and arbitration in the event of a dispute.

Figure 6-1. Sample Job Offer Letter

Date
Name
Address

Dear _____:

It is my pleasure to extend the following offer of employment to you on behalf of X Company. This offer is contingent upon your passing our mandatory drug screen, our receipt of your college transcripts, etc.

Title:_____

Reporting Relationship: The position will report to:

_____

Job Description is attached.

Base Salary: Will be paid in biweekly installments of $_____, which is equivalent to $_____ on an annual basis, and subject to deductions for taxes and other withholdings as required by law or the policies of the company.

Bonus (or Commission) Potential: Effective upon satisfactory completion of the first 90 days of employment, and based upon the goals and objectives agreed to in the performance development planning process with your manager, you may be eligible for a bonus.

Noncompete Agreement: Our standard noncompete agreement must be signed prior to start.

Benefits: The current, standard company health, life, disability, and dental insurance coverages are generally supplied per company policy. Eligibility for other benefits, including the 401(k) and tuition reimbursement, will generally take place per company policy. Employee contribution to payment for benefit plans is determined annually.

Stock Options: Spell out any options that may be available for purchase.

Vacation and Personal Emergency Time Off: Vacation is accrued at X hours per pay period, which is equivalent to two weeks on an annual basis. Personal emergency days are generally accrued per company policy.

Expenses: Spell out any moving or other transition expenses the company will pay.

Start Date: _____

Car/Phone/Travel Expenses: Normal and reasonable expenses will be reimbursed on a monthly basis per company policy.

Your employment with X Company is at-will and either party can terminate the relationship at any time with or without cause and with or without notice.

You acknowledge that this offer letter (along with the final form of any referenced documents) represents the entire agreement between you and X Company and that no verbal or written agreements, promises, or representations that are not specifically stated in this offer are or will be binding upon X Company.

If you are in agreement with the above outline, please sign below. This offer is in effect for five business days.

Signatures:

_____
(For X Company)

_____
Date

_____
(For Candidate)

_____
Date

This sample job offer letter was provided by Susan Heathfield (2005) at About.com.

According to Nolo (2007), a legal information provider, there is no law that will tell you when to ask a new employee to sign a written employment contract, nor are there any hard and fast rules. The only thing that can be said for certain is that employment contracts are not for everyone or for every situation. Nolo suggests that in making a decision, you weigh the advantages and disadvantages, which include the following.

Advantages:

- An employment contract can be beneficial in circumstances where you want control over the employee's ability to leave your business. If the employee is a high-level manager or executive, or if the employee is especially valuable to your business, then a contract can protect you from the sudden, unexpected loss of the employee. It can lock the employee into a specific term or it can require the employee to give you enough notice to find and train a suitable replacement.

Figure 6-2. Sample Confidentiality Agreement

This Agreement is entered into this ___ day of _____, 200__, by and between _____ with offices at _____ (hereinafter "Recipient") and _____, with offices at _____ (hereinafter "Discloser").

WHEREAS Discloser possesses certain ideas and information relating to _____ that is confidential and proprietary to Discloser (hereinafter "Confidential Information"); and

WHEREAS the Recipient is willing to receive disclosure of the Confidential Information pursuant to the terms of this Agreement for the purpose of _____;

NOW THEREFORE, in consideration for the mutual undertakings of the Discloser and the Recipient under this Agreement, the parties agree as follows:

1. Disclosure. Discloser agrees to disclose, and Receiver agrees to receive the Confidential Information.

2. Confidentiality.

2.1 No Use. Recipient agrees not to use the Confidential Information in any way, or to manufacture or test any product embodying Confidential Information, except for the purpose set forth above.

2.2 No Disclosure. Recipient agrees to use its best efforts to prevent and protect the Confidential Information, or any part thereof, from disclosure to any person other than Recipient's employees having a need for disclosure in connection with Recipient's authorized use of the Confidential Information.

2.3 Protection of Secrecy. Recipient agrees to take all steps reasonably necessary to protect the secrecy of the Confidential Information, and to prevent the Confidential Information from falling into the public domain or into the possession of unauthorized persons.

3. Limits on Confidential Information. Confidential Information shall not be deemed proprietary and the Recipient shall have no obligation with respect to such information where the information:

(a) Was known to Recipient prior to receiving any of the Confidential Information from Discloser;

(b) Has become publicly known through no wrongful act of Recipient;

(c) Was received by Recipient without breach of this Agreement from a third party without restriction as to the use and disclosure of the information;

(d) Was independently developed by Recipient without use of the Confidential Information; or

(e) Was ordered to be publicly released by the requirement of a government agency.

4. Ownership of Confidential Information. Recipient agrees that all Confidential Information shall remain the property of Discloser, and that Discloser may use such Confidential Information for any purpose without obligation to Recipient. Nothing contained herein shall be construed as granting or implying any transfer of rights to Recipient in the Confidential Information, or any patents or other intellectual property protecting or relating to the Confidential Information.

5. Term and Termination. The obligations of this Agreement shall be continuing until the Confidential Information disclosed to Recipient is no longer confidential.

6. Survival of Rights and Obligations. This Agreement shall be binding upon, inure to the benefit of, and be enforceable by (a) Discloser, its successors, and assigns; and (b) Recipient, its successors, and assigns.

IN WITNESS WHEREOF, the parties have executed this agreement effective as of the date first written above.

DISCLOSER (_____) RECIPIENT (_____)

Signed: _____ Signed: _____

Print Name: _____ Print Name: _____

Title:_____ Title:_____

Date: _____ Date: _____

This sample Confidentiality Agreement was provided by Daniel A. Tysver of Beck & Tysver PLLC (2007) in Minneapolis. It is intended as general information only and is not intended to serve as legal advice or as a substitute for legal counsel.

- If the employee will be learning confidential and sensitive information about your business, you can insert confidentiality clauses that prevent the employee from disclosing the information or using it for personal gain (see figure 6-2 for a standalone confidentiality agreement).
- An employment contract can prevent the employee from competing against you after leaving your company (also see figure 6-3 for a standalone non-compete agreement). Keep in mind, however, that noncompete clauses or agreements are often difficult to enforce and are not looked favorably upon by the courts because they restrict an individual's employment options.

Figure 6-3. Sample Noncompete Agreement

For good consideration and as an inducement for_____(Company) to employ_____(Employee), the undersigned.

Employee hereby agrees not to directly or indirectly compete with the business of the Company and its successors and assigns during the period of employment and for a period of _____ years following termination of employment and notwithstanding the cause or reason for termination.

The term "not compete" as used herein shall mean that the Employee shall not own, manage, operate, consult, or be an employee in a business substantially similar to or competitive with the present business of the Company or such other business activity in which the Company may substantially engage during the term of employment.

The Employee acknowledges that the Company shall or may in reliance of this agreement provide Employee access to trade secrets, customers, and other confidential data and goodwill. Employee agrees to retain said information as confidential and not to use said information on his or her own behalf or disclose same to any third party.

This agreement shall be binding upon and inure to the benefit of the parties, their successors, assigns, and personal representatives.

Signed this _____ day of _____ 20____.

_____
Company

_____
Employee

This sample Noncompete Agreement was provided by Kinsey Law Offices (Kinsey 2007). It is intended as general information only and is not intended to serve as legal advice or as a substitute for legal counsel.

- You can use an employment contract as a way to entice a highly skilled individual to come work for you instead of the competition. By promising the individual job security and beneficial terms in an employment contract, you can, says Nolo, "sweeten the deal."
- If the contract specifies standards for the employee's performance and grounds for termination, you may have an easier time terminating an employee who doesn't live up to your standards.

Disadvantages:

- An employment contract binds both you and the employee, which, says Nolo, might pose a problem if you later decide that you don't like the contract terms and want to get out of them. The employment contract limits your ability to alter the terms of employment if the needs of your business change. The only way to change the terms of the contract is to renegotiate them.
- A contract brings with it the obligation to deal fairly with the employee. In legal terms, this is called the "covenant of good faith and fair dealing." If you end up treating the employee in a way that seems unfair, you may find yourself in court.

If you decide that, for whatever reason, an employment contract is not the way to go, then you want to make sure you're not making any statements in your offer package that could be interpreted as contractual language. The *Business Owner's Toolkit* (2007; Toolkit.com) says that because employment-at-will laws in most states give you wide latitude if you need to fire an employee, you don't want to throw away that privilege by inadvertently giving special rights to the candidate. To prevent this, the *Business Owner's Toolkit* suggests that your offer be stated as narrowly as possible, avoiding

- statements that designate employees as "permanent," which allude to long-term job security
- statements such as "you will have a long, rewarding, and satisfying career ahead of you" and "we will pay one-half your moving expenses now and the balance after one year," which could be construed as meaning that the employment relationship was intended to be at least a year long
- statements that are open to interpretation and can land you in court if the employee isn't working out and you decide to let him or her go ("you'll be with us as long as you can do your job," "you will not be fired without just cause," or "this is a company in which you can stay and grow").

The *Business Owner's Toolkit* also recommends reviewing all job advertisements and company literature for language that could be interpreted as offering employment of a fixed duration, including phrases like "our company family," "job security," and "lack of layoffs." Furthermore, take a second look at your interview notes to determine whether any promises were made that need to be corrected in the formal offer letter.

For more on how to handle the candidates you don't hire, see the sidebar.

Letting Other Candidates Down Easy

Once your first choice has accepted the job, how do you close the loop with the other candidates? My first piece of advice is to contact them and let them know of your decision. This may sound obvious, but it's shocking how many organizations don't do it and just leave candidates hanging. If a candidate takes the time to interview with you, you at least owe him or her the courtesy of a phone call or email.

I've heard that official rejection letters on company letterhead are rather out of vogue, and if you have met a candidate in person, it's probably best to follow up by phone. "I always call candidates who interview in person and thank them for their time and interest and let them know that we are not planning to move forward at this time," says staffing consultant and executive coach Simon Meth (2007). "Rather than giving reasons, just thank them for their time and interest." For candidates whom you've screened by phone and won't be pursuing further, send an email that conveys the same message.

Steering away from giving reasons is one thing, but you also want to end your interaction with a rejected candidate on a positive note. You never know who the applicant knows, or when you might run into or be in the position of working with him or her again. For example, a few years ago a colleague of mine treated a new college graduate applicant pretty poorly, stringing her along for weeks on end. He sincerely regretted his behavior when the graduate eventually became his client.

Some hiring managers just don't get around to either a phone call or an email, citing the fact that they're too busy and can't keep track of all the people they interview. But by letting candidates know where they stand, you'll actually save time because they won't be checking in repeatedly regarding the status of an offer. And, as Meth points out, this approach is "clean and doesn't have any legal ramifications."

The Preorientation Orientation

Your candidate has signed on the dotted line and is now your employee! While the hiring experience is still fresh in your mind, get together with your selection committee and do a postmortem in which you consider the effectiveness of the process you've just undertaken. Did everything go as smoothly as possible? Were there any slipups or inefficiencies that could be prevented next time around?

If there are a few weeks between the day a candidate accepts your offer and the day he or she reports to work, you should make an effort to keep in touch. "Offer-making is like proposing—you can't stop dating and still expect them to say yes," says Tom Gimbel, founder and CEO of the LaSalle Network. "Retreating is the worst thing you can do. You've worked hard to connect with this individual, now close the deal. Contact the candidate and see where his head is at. A deal breaker could very well be a small thing to fix."

Gerry Crispin, author of *Career XRoads,* suggests creating a series of touch points to integrate the new hire into the company and work team even while she is wrapping up her other job. Are you her immediate supervisor? Perhaps send her some relevant reading and/or materials so she can get up to speed on the business. It may also be appropriate to invite her to virtually participate in a team meeting so that you can introduce her to people in your group she hasn't met yet. "You could also," says Crispin, "cc her on emails, ask her opinion on a specific issue, meet at a trade show, or take the family out while they come in on a house-shopping trip." If the new employee reports to someone else, connect her with that person and arrange a wel-come meeting or lunch, or at the very least a phone conversation.

Your next step should be to prepare a valuable new hire orientation for your new employee's first day, an event that's the subject of chapter 7.

Making It Happen

As you prepare to seal the deal, step up your efforts to sell the candidate on your organization, including arranging social outings or employee meet-and-greets. Also:

- Make your verbal offer in person or via phone, on a Monday morning—providing an overview of the job, the compensation, and the next steps.
- Send an offer in writing confirming the details (that is, the proposed start date, job title and responsibilities, compensation, and decision deadline).
- Weigh the pros and cons of using an employment contract, because such agreements are not for every situation.
- Keep in touch with your new hire before his or her start date by sending him or her relevant reading material or inviting him or her to participate in a team meeting.

Improve New Hire Orientation: Help Employees Start on the Right Foot—and Reap the Benefits

.... **In this chapter, you'll learn to** ....

- create a structured orientation process that reduces both startup costs and employee anxiety and turnover
- implement goodwill gestures that celebrate the new hire
- include longer-term activities such as one-to-one meetings and satisfaction surveys
- deliver consistent messages to a geographically dispersed workforce via web-based programs.

When I think of new hire orientations of jobs past, I remember watching cheesy, outdated videos, completing a marathon of poorly photocopied forms, and being escorted to an empty cubicle three hours before the end of the business day, left to wonder how I should pass the time until my new boss got back from an offsite meeting. I remember thinking about how homesick I was for the job I'd just left, how I had this sick feeling in my stomach, how I feared I'd made a terrible mistake.

My experiences are not unique. Despite notable innovations in other areas of human resources, the new hire orientation continues to be an overlooked area. And if you think about all the time and effort you just spent to bring the new hire onboard in the first place, this doesn't make sense. If your orientation makes an off-putting impression, it may take months to overcome the bad taste the new employee now has in his mouth.

Poor orientations also slow time to productivity, increase error rates, and have an adverse impact on recruitment efforts. "Everyone you know asks you during your first week 'How's your new job?'" says Judith Brown, human resources specialist at McNeil Technologies, Inc. "Unfortunately, the response to the question is often 'It's not what I expected' or 'they never told me . . .,' which can result in negative rumors that discourage others from applying."

Improving orientation can increase retention rates by as much as 25 percent. "An effective orientation has a great impact on the new employee's job satisfaction," says Matt Curran, vice president at Executive Staffing Group. "An employee who gets off on the right foot is more likely to have better job performance and to want to stay on the job longer." In this chapter, we'll discuss how you can design your orientation program in a way that drives forward a new employee's successful acclimation into your business.

Orientation Goals: More Than Goodwill

The first step in turning around your new hire orientation is to realize that it's not just a formality or something you do as a goodwill gesture. Judith Brown tells us that best orientations are created strategically to achieve these objectives:

- *Reduce startup costs.* Proper orientation can help the employee get up to speed much more quickly, thereby reducing the costs associated with learning the job.
- *Reduce anxiety.* Any employee, when put into a new, strange situation, will experience anxiety that can impede her ability to learn the job. Proper orientation helps to reduce anxiety that results from entering into an unknown situation and helps provide guidelines for behavior and conduct, so the employee doesn't have to experience the stress of guessing.

- *Reduce employee turnover.* Employee turnover increases as employees feel they are not valued or are put in positions where they can't possibly do their jobs. Orientation shows that the organization values the employee and helps provide the tools necessary for succeeding in the job.
- *Save time for the supervisor.* Simply put, the better the initial orientation, the less likely supervisors and co-workers will have to spend time teaching the employee.
- *Develop realistic job expectations.* It is important that employees learn as soon as possible what is expected of them and what to expect from others, in addition to learning about the values and attitudes of the organization.

Well-thought-out orientations also celebrate the arrival of the new hire, integrate him into the team, provide a comfortable forum for answering questions that extends beyond the first day, and involve customized programs that meet your new employee's unique needs.

Setting the Tone

Like the hiring process you just undertook, the orientation process should begin well before the new hire arrives for her first day. In chapter 6, we talked about how to bridge the time between offer acceptance and start date. Two issues to keep in mind as you prepare to officially welcome your new employee are the owner and tone of the orientation.

Orientation owner. Although new hire orientations are typically managed by junior-level human resources staff, these people should not be responsible for assimilating a new employee. Orientations should be designed and run by the new hire's manager and peers, because who better understands exactly what needs to be done to get this person up to speed? The human resources department can have a standard one- or two-hour session to sign paperwork and go over corporate policies and benefits, but beyond that, the new employee's department should be running the show.

Orientation tone. The whole organization should be involved in creating the perception that a new hire is something to be celebrated. "Consider the experience from the employee's perspective, and then make an effort to make it as fun and painless as possible," says Brian Platz, executive vice president and general manager at Silk

Road Technology, a web-based talent management solutions provider. "If you do, you will make your new team member feel valued, wanted, interested, and excited. By engendering these positive emotions from the word go, you make the new employee want to do great work and add great value to your organization."

John Sullivan (1998), professor of human resource management at San Francisco State University's College of Business, believes that the following gestures go a long way in setting the right tone for a new hire:

- *Involve the CEO or general manager:* Encourage a high-level executive to stop by your new employee's office, send a personal email, or make a phone call welcoming the employee to the organization. Francie Dalton, president of Dalton Alliances, agrees with this suggestion. "Ideally, the CEO would conduct part of the orientation, including specifics about how the individual's function contributes to overall organizational success," she says. "When the CEO takes the time to do this, it can be inspirational, underscoring how valuable the individual is perceived to be by the organization."

- *Plan a special outing:* Take the team out to lunch on the new hire's first day, organize a dinner with other new employees and their spouses, or engage in a team-building activity with current employees. "I recommend experiential, hands-on learning that shows people how important teams are to success," adds Chris Musselwhite, president and CEO of Discovery Learning. "My company, for example, has a team-building simulation called Paper Planes, which has been shown to have a dramatic impact on new hires' impressions of company culture."

- *Make an announcement:* Place a welcome note and picture on the company intranet, and if many staff read the local paper or company e-newsletter, put a notice in to let everyone know about your new team member.

- *Get creative with the new hire's office space:* Have your administrative assistant create a banner signed by the team, or hang a team picture on the wall.

- *Gift them little extras:* Send the new hire's spouse and kids first day welcome gifts, corporate products, or cards to make them feel they are part of the team and to build support for the new company.

Rome Wasn't Built in a Day

Personal touches like the ones described above should motivate new employees as you begin the process of showing them how things are done in your organization and providing them with the tools to do their jobs effectively. A critical point is that orientations need not be limited to one day. Ideally, activities should be planned over the course of a few weeks so that you don't overwhelm the new hire or neglect important things he or she needs to know. Use the new hire checklist in figure 7-1 to keep track of all the moving parts!

Human Resources Session

Your streamlined human resources session should be the part of orientation where you address housekeeping issues related to employment in your organization. It should include a brief history of the organization's history and culture, an overview of the Employee Handbook, and an explanation of benefits. It's also a good time to ensure that the most critical paperwork is signed. Small businesses in particular should keep in mind that the Internal Revenue Service Form W-4, which specifies income tax withholding, and U.S. Citizenship and Immigration Services Form I-9, which demonstrates that the employee is eligible to work in the United States, are required for every new hire. If these forms are not filled out completely and accurately, your organization could be subjected to harsh penalties.

In the interest of time and keeping your new hire engaged, only the essential documentation should be addressed in the human resources session. "For everything else, create an online hub where new hires can find materials as they need them," says Brian Platz. "Once they've settled into their new job, send a reminder email that certain materials are available online."

Systems Setup

One of the most common complaints I hear from new employees is that nothing—not their office, their computer, or their phone—is set up when they arrive. "A senior-level, highly technical internal auditor was hired for a long-term project to clean some things up in the company's financial statements," relates Tom Gimbel, founder and CEO of the LaSalle Network. "When the candidate showed up for work on the first day, he found himself in an office with no computer, no office

Figure 7-1. New Hire Checklist

Name _____

Department_____

Supervisor _____

Start Date _____

Date/Location for HR Session _____

Date/Location for Welcome Event _____

Welcome Announcement Plans

HR Session Attendance _____

Tax and Benefits Paperwork Completed _____

Employee Handbook/Policy Manual Delivered _____

Organization-Specific Orientation Materials Delivered _____

Office Assigned_____

Computer Systems Required/Setup

Supplies Required/Ordered

One-to-One Meetings

Individual	Date/Time/Location	Purpose

Scheduled Training

Scheduled Follow-up

supplies, and no direction to take regarding the assignment. He was asked to complete some work in an Excel spreadsheet that he wound up starting by using a hand-held calculator. Fed up and frustrated, he left the assignment and the managers had no idea why. The core lesson here? Have your ducks in a row."

It shouldn't be that difficult to stock your new hire's office with supplies, and get the information systems up and running so that there is an email address, a phone extension, identification card, and access to various company applications and online resources waiting for him or her. You should also have business cards printed in advance so that he or she can use them when meeting other employees.

New Hire 411

In addition to the standard company information that human resources will provide, the hiring manager may wish to put together an orientation package with items such as these recommended by John Sullivan:

- Your department or group's short-term plan and organizational chart
- Glossary of acronyms, buzzwords, and list of frequently asked questions so your new hire doesn't have to ask uncomfortable questions about what things mean
- A "Help Source" card with the names and contact information of people who the new hire can tap for assistance
- Team photographs so it will be easier for the new employee to match names to faces, or a "who's who" compilation on your intranet site.

One-to-One Meetings

Helping your new hire to develop strong relationships with key players throughout the organization should be a top orientation priority. "Many people spend more time at work than they do with their friends and family," says Lori Blackman, president of DNL Global, a recruitment firm in the global services industry. "An emotional connection develops when new employees really get to know their co-workers and create friendships with others in the workplace."

To facilitate this, preschedule meetings with various team members throughout the first two weeks, assigning each employee to cover specific items. I always liked the idea of setting the new employee up with a recently hired mentor in another department. And make sure the new employee's supervisor is available to meet with him or her on the first day, and is also readily accessible during the orientation period. Finally, John Sullivan offers these creative tips for facilitating one-on-one interaction: "Give the new hire $25 gift certificates for the five employees who help him the most during his first week, and/or give him 'free lunch' coupons to take co-workers out to local restaurants."

Training Sessions

We will talk more about training and development in the next chapter, but for the purpose of orientation, you should discuss the new hire's immediate needs with him before his start date. If relevant courses are given internally or hosted online, schedule them to occur as soon as possible. Develop a growth plan for the new employee's first three to six months in which you include key projects he can start working on right away.

Orientation Follow-up

Even organizations that do a good job with structured orientations sometimes fall down when it comes to keeping an open dialogue with the new hire. Either a hiring manager or human resources professional should be touching base with the employee every few months to assess how well she is assimilating and to mitigate any problems or frustrations. John Sullivan also suggests doing a postorientation survey asking participants what they want more of (and less of) with respect to orientation. Prompt them to write down any new ideas or solutions they have on how to improve orientation—and then use them.

For more on onboarding do's and don'ts, see the sidebar.

Online Orientation: Information How and When People Need It

Online orientation methods have gained traction in the last five years, but mostly with large, global organizations that need to be able to deliver consistent messages to a geographically dispersed workforce. In today's world, however, nearly all organizations should be leveraging at least some web-based technology to provide information where and when new employees need it.

Onboarding Dos and Don'ts

"Onboarding," the human resources term for integrating a new employee into the organizational culture, is a delicate process. In addition to the orientation recommendations described in this chapter, here are some dos and don'ts to consider:

- **Do** *put "need to knows" at a convenient, regularly updated online location.* "Post new employee orientation schedules, materials, benefits forms, and an extensive FAQ about the company on an intranet that is accessible to new hires from a welcome email before their first day on the job," says Brian Platz, executive vice president and general manager at Silk Road Technology. "By providing some information in advance, you eliminate a common source of new hire angst."

- **Don't** *have the new hire start during a week when her manager is either out of town or insanely busy with a project deadline.* This will give the new employee a feeling of being disconnected and will leave her with too much time on her hands to sit in her office and stare at the four walls.

- **Do** *plan who your new hire meets in his first few days strategically.* The employees you want the new guy to be hanging out with are friendly, positive about the organization, and happy with their work.

- **Don't** *keep your new employee waiting around on his first day.* "The worst thing to do," says About.com's Susan Heathfield (2007b), "is to leave him standing in the lobby for a half hour while reception staff tries to figure out what to do with him."

- **Do** *fully leverage the technology available to you.* Although there is no replacing personal interactions, some onboarding messages can be delivered using computer-based simulations and e-learning.

- **Don't** *make your new hire learn the hard way how things are done.* "Every workplace comes with its own set of rules and regulations, nuances, and traditions," says Brian Platz. "For example, if your organization observes a casual Friday rule, make sure the new hire knows this before showing up at the office on her first Friday in a neatly pressed suit."

- **Do** *ensure that the employee has ample time to complete orientation activities while also getting immersed in his new job.* "Neither can be put on hold," says Heathfield (2007a). "My current new director spent the morning helping to write an RFP for a potential customer rather than attending his scheduled meetings. I didn't want his orientation to get off track, but this activity was ideal for helping him integrate quickly into the working business of the company."

According to Leanne Johnson and Roberta Westwood (2002), who wrote about online orientation in ASTD *Infoline*, benefits include better employee preparedness, support for and assimilation into organizational culture, flexibility and convenience, compressed delivery time, ability to test for understanding, reduced workload for staff and trainers, and ease of updating. Most online orientation methods are focused around the organization's intranet site and may include any or all of these features:

- personal guides and virtual tours
- descriptions of and messaging around the organization's vision, mission, and values
- interactive organizational charts
- current employee stories and photos
- departmental mini-websites
- web-based employee handbook, benefits information, and human resources forms
- demonstrations of executive leadership and commitment
- e-learning and guided research activities
- games and simulations
- social networking tools, wikis, or discussion boards
- email groups or list-servs
- orientation meeting and training session setup
- online mentoring programs
- video and audio clips
- case studies.

Many organizations choose to develop a new employee orientation website or web portal to house the features listed above. The best orientation websites are creative, interesting, and memorable, displaying a unified theme that reflects the organizational culture. Johnson and Westwood say that they also:

- are process oriented and designed to be used over an extended period via modules with a number of activities
- are up to date and in line with the promising impression made during the recruitment process
- are designed to be inclusive, addressing the needs of all employees from frontline workers to senior executives.

Intel Case Study

"Learn about the company, the culture, and your role." This is the purpose of Intel's new employee orientation website. Upon entering the site, new employees immediately meet Tamiko, their tour guide. Tamiko adds a special and personal touch to Intel's online orientation. She greets new hires, acts as their companion throughout the orientation, and is a virtual "someone to go to" when they are seeking information. Features of the Intel NEO site include

- my action plan
- my site and organization
- managers of new hires
- classroom materials
- online modules.

With 80,000 employees worldwide, Intel needed an orientation program that was flexible, modular, and scalable for use globally. The design process reflected the diverse culture of the organization, and the site was developed so that it would be easy for regions to customize.

The imagery reflecting orientation at Intel was carefully planned to tie in with recruiting materials. Orientation actually begins long before hiring, with a description of values on the recruitment page of Intel's public website. The emphasis on the company's values is critical, because they are the foundation of Intel's culture. Transitioning key information online has allowed Intel to make the most of face-to-face orientation workshops. Other elements of Intel's blended new employee orientation include

- a welcome envelope
- a two- to four-hour new employee session held weekly
- a teleconference call option for remote, geographically dispersed new hires
- working at Intel: A daylong culture class that includes a question-and-answer session with a senior manager.

This case study was provided by ASTD InfoLine (Johnson and Westwood 2002).

Because the costs of implementing an online orientation program can run any-where from a few thousand to a few hundred thousand dollars, you should care-fully assess the needs of your organization before getting started. This will likely include activities such as holding cross-departmental brainstorms, auditing exist-ing orientation programs, and conducting focus groups with recent hires. "I am a fan of doing a reality TV type of confessional booth arrangement where a hiring manager can gather the internal dialogues of employees and hear their opinions of new hire orientation," says Kevin Fleming, president and CEO of Effective Executive Coaching. "I think most managers will be blown away by what people really think and the creative solutions that are offered."

At the conclusion of your research, you'll want to identify top priorities, outline goals for your online orientation program, decide on strategies to address those goals, and determine how you will evaluate their effectiveness. Documents such as the one in figure 7-2 can be helpful as you undertake the planning process.

Your preparation must also designate an internal team that can chaperone the effort from start to finish, employing any outside resources (technology vendors and the like) that may be necessary. And from the beginning, you should also keep in mind that online orientation methods are best used in conjunction with classroom or meeting-based activities that emphasize personal interaction (see the Intel Case Study sidebar).

Making It Happen

Poor orientations slow time to productivity, increase error rates, and have an adverse impact on recruitment efforts. You can increase your staff retention by up to 25 percent by implementing these best practices:

- Arrange for orientations to be designed and run by the new hire's manager and peers.
- Plan activities over the course of a few weeks so that you don't overwhelm the new hire or neglect important things he or she needs to know.
- Help your new hire to develop strong relationships with key players throughout the organization.
- Support easy assimilation of large numbers of new hires by including an online component such as a new employee website or web portal.

Figure 7-2. Online Orientation Worksheet

Use this worksheet to ensure that you have addressed all the variables involved in creating and implementing online new employee orientation.

The Business Case

Does a complete online orientation make sense for our organization? For example, do we have:

- A medium-to-large workforce?
- A geographically dispersed workforce?
- Staggered start dates?
- Intranet technology in place?

What are the goals and benefits of online orientation? What do we hope to achieve, and how will we know if we are successful?

What are our top priorities when it comes to online orientation?

The Blend

How do we plan to use online orientation in conjunction with group orientation sessions?

What other activities and tools will be part of the overall new employee orientation blend?

Online Culture

How can online orientation reflect our culture?

Internal Planning

Who will be on the team and champion the effort internally? Who will ensure that online orientation has executive support?

What sources can we tap during data collection (exit interviews, evaluation information from existing orientation program, stakeholder and recent hire focus groups, etc.)?

Design Principles

How will the following universal new employee orientation principles be reflected in the online orientation?

- Is it part of the recruitment process?
- Does it have a link to the culture and values of our organization?

(continued on next page)

Figure 7-2. Online Orientation Worksheet (continued)

- Does it include the involvement of executives, human resources, managers, and mentors?
- Is it fresh and memorable, and does it create an "experience" for the new hire?
- It is a process and not an event?
- Does it make a good and lasting first impression?
- Is it inclusive?

Learning Technologies

What learning technologies will we utilize in the development of our online orientation?

- Orientation website
- Individual web pages
- Self-paced online learning
- Discussion forums, social networking tools, wikis, and email
- Webinars.

Design Considerations

Do the development plans for a new site adequately address the following considerations?

- What will the unifying theme be?
- Will the new site have a conversational tone?
- Will it have intuitive navigation?
- Will it avoid regurgitating intranet information?
- Will it make use of existing tools?
- Will it address language issues?
- Will it contain divisional orientation sites?
- Will it contain plans for evaluation?

Design Features

What functionality should we incorporate into the online orientation program?

Access

Who will have access to the new employee orientation website?

- New full-time employees
- New part-time employees
- New temporary employees
- Employees returning from extended leave
- Existing employees.

Access (continued)

Who will have access to the new employee orientation website?

- Managers
- Contractors
- Customers
- Others.

How will the online orientation website be accessed (from the office, from home, from mobile devices, etc.)?

How will we ensure access for employees who do not use computers as part of their regular jobs?

How will we inform new employees about the website and how to access it?

Implementation

Who will help us to develop and implement the new website (information technology department, vendor, etc.)?

What are the budget parameters for this project?

How will we select an appropriate vendor, if necessary?

How will we ensure that managers and employees have a clear understanding of their roles with regard to online orientation?

What is the timeline and roll-out plan for the new online program?

Develop Strong Training and Growth Plans: Empower New Employees with a Culture of Learning

---

In this chapter, you'll learn to

- assess your current environment with a comprehensive training needs analysis
- design formal courses that will facilitate training an entire population of new hires
- develop a customized 90-day training plan as well as a long-term plan for every new employee
- implement mentoring programs that show new hires you're committed to their growth.

I've never had the experience of working full time for an organization that did employee training and development particularly well. I think I know why. In today's world, corporate loyalty is a thing of the past, and some people switch jobs more frequently than they change their wardrobe. Many organizations may feel uncomfortable about spending buckets of time and resources helping employees to develop important transferrable skills, only to see them contribute their newfound knowledge to a competitor's bottom line.

Fortunately, most organizations are starting to realize the inherent value of having a culture focused on learning. "Both individuals and organizations benefit from well-defined training and growth plans," says David Hyatt, president of CorVirtus. "Having appropriate processes in place to develop people in the right way increases competitive ability and motivation. The positive reputation derived from such an approach also increases the potential to recruit capable people and ensure that you become an employer of choice."

This chapter explores how to create training and growth plans for your new hires, including assessing current offerings, developing workable course designs, customizing programs according to individual employee needs, and facilitating mentoring in your organization.

Know Your Organization: Training Needs Analysis

Though your natural instinct might be to dive into planning right away, you want your employee training decisions to be informed by knowledge of your organization's needs. Intulogy, a provider of outsource training services, provides four basic steps to help you assess your current environment:

1. *Analyze your situation:* Too often, businesses opt for too little, too late when it comes to employee training, leaving their people with incomplete or inappropriate solutions. You can prevent this from happening by zeroing in on the most critical questions about your business processes, your employees' skill acquisition, and the training tactics that will handily address both—right at the start. In listing some of these questions and providing room for your responses, the worksheet in figure 8-1 will help to crystallize your thoughts.

2. *Evaluate the training in place:* Even if your company hasn't formalized new hire training, you probably have some relevant materials developed already, especially if you've just coordinated the type of new hire orientation discussed in the last chapter. Background documents—including employee manuals, product and service overviews, and process charts—should be incorporated into any and all new training plans.

3. *Identify gaps:* You'll want to inventory existing internal resources to see who and what you'll be able to leverage for any new training initiatives. By identifying what your organization can and cannot provide, you'll learn exactly what you'll need when looking for assistance. For example, if you think you might want to

Figure 8-1. Training Needs Analysis Worksheet

Date _____

Prepared by _____

Title _____

Department _____

Current New Hire Training Budget (ASTD estimates that U.S. corporations spend 2 percent of payroll on employee training): _____

Proposed New Hire Training Budget: _____

Current New Hire Training Activities and Materials (at company and department levels)

Perceived Quality of Current Activities and Materials

Effectiveness of Current Activities and Materials

Business Processes and Employee Skills Audit

How do our employees currently learn? Does our staff have the skills they need to do their jobs?

Are there any business needs that are not being met? How can we better align new hire training to these needs?

Are we making any major changes in our business process? What impact do those changes have on our employees' job functions?

Tactical "Wish List"

Potential Internal Resources to Call On

Potential External Resources to Call On

utilize e-learning, you could first check with your information technology team to see if it could develop a solution in-house. If this won't work, tap those team members to help you determine project requirements for an outside vendor.

4. *Assess your options:* The larger your organization, the more likely it is that you will be able to take advantage of internal resources. If you do decide to look outside, however, consider these questions: Does this company or individual have a proven track record of satisfied customers? Will they work well with your business culture? Will they be able to fill in all the gaps you have identified? Can they provide you with multiple training options?

Creating Your New Training Mix

Once you've assessed your training needs, you'll be ready to start planning your implementation. Because this book is primarily about developing relationships with potential and new employees, we focus here on new hire training. Regardless of the delivery method, this type of training should provide core information about the organization's policies, procedures, departments, resources, performance expectations, and necessary skills. Ideally, an offline or online employee manual that is both conversational and informative should serve as the backbone of your new hire training. Now let's take a look at some of the more frequently used components of a new hire training mix.

Formal Course Design

When you need to train an entire population of new hires—whether on a specialized computer system or a century's worth of company history—a formal course design may be the way to go. Intulogy compares this exercise to building a new house, for which you would want to make sure that the architect provides the builder with a clear set of blueprints that creates your dream home. Once you've identified your training needs and goals with the needs analysis, you might follow Intulogy's (2007b) five instructional design steps to develop your course (and see the Intulogy Case Study sidebar):

1. *Determine the entry behaviors of participants.* It's important to consider what the learners already know and how they will approach the material, so you'll need to identify the skills, knowledge, and attitudes an average participant can be expected to possess at the beginning of the course.

Intulogy Case Study

A leading provider of conference communications solutions depended on its call center operators to provide both contact and services to clients. With over 12,000 clients relying on them for telephone and Internet conference solutions, the company needed to ensure that its call center operators received high-quality systems and strong customer service training.

The firm's senior managers believed that operator training was essential to the company's continued growth and success. They chose Intulogy to design and develop the firm's call center training solution. After a thorough needs analysis, Intulogy determined that the firm could benefit from more than just new training materials. Consultants provided the following services:

- *Training design and development:* Intulogy designed and developed a complete call center training curriculum for new hire and expert operator audiences.

- *Train-the-trainer delivery:* After the training was complete, Intulogy consultants delivered a train-the-trainer course to the company's in-house classroom instructors and execution floor instructors, providing assistance in making the training successful.

- *Error reduction:* In the training development process, Intulogy focused on reducing the number of operator errors to improve quality of service and customer satisfaction.

- *Management consulting:* Intulogy provided the company's managers with recommendations for streamlining their training organization to better meet their future training needs and costs.

The company's operators receive customer service and systems training in a simulated execution floor. They practice greeting callers, placing them into conference calls, and handling special requests. This hands-on practice allows operators to gain confidence before working on the operations floor.

The director of the call center training initiative praises Intulogy: "They have been instrumental in creating instructor and participant manuals for us, enabling us to offer more professional and detailed training." She also praises the train-the-trainer sessions, because they have made it possible for the call center to "provide consistent training in all classes in both our facilities."

This case study was provided by Intulogy (2007a).

2. *Set performance and learning objectives.* Then, you'll want to assess what skills, knowledge, and attitudes the learners need to achieve through the course. Write learning objectives that define a task, a context, or a situation, and a measure of success. Some of Intulogy's examples include: The supervisor can conduct annual performance reviews based on company guidelines. The technician can use current procedures for the nightly backup of system records. The sales representative can accurately enter all fields in the new customer profile within five minutes. The course's goals are critical to its success. To ensure that your participants really understand and can apply a concept, your learning objectives must lead to actions that you can observe and measure.

3. *Build the training outline.* Individual training steps should take your participants from their entry behaviors to the completion of the learning objectives, with each step building upon the previous steps.

4. *Create performance assessments.* Consider how an instructor or supervisor can determine whether the participant has met the learning objective. A learner may be asked to demonstrate a skill, identify the correct action, or apply the knowledge.

5. *Select program format.* Evaluate the possible methods of training delivery, including classroom-style or online.

Online Courses

According to Harvard Business Essentials' (2002) *Hiring and Keeping the Best People*, although online training is seldom a complete solution because of the lack of personal interaction, it has clear advantages over formal classroom training, including lower cost to supply, elimination of travel costs and lost production time, scalability to any level of demand, and on-demand availability.

Taking training online is really just as simple as using a web-conferencing solution. Your materials will be similar to what you would use for a live classroom session and might include PowerPoint presentations, handouts, surveys, and tests. Keep in mind these tips for making the best use of online training features:

- Make PowerPoints digestible, with small blocks of text and interesting visuals.
- Emphasize points by using the highlighter and pointer tools.

- Alternate between the PowerPoint presentation and a live demonstration on a desktop application or website.
- Track your results by conducting online surveys, question-and-answer sessions, and polls.

Most organizations will require at least some vendor assistance in rolling out a web-conferencing solution—although, in your needs analysis, you may have discovered systems that are already in place. For example, in speaking with your investor relations team, you may learn that they are using web conferencing to broadcast quarterly earnings results to their shareholders. In a case like this, it very well might be easier to extend the existing solution so that it's also appropriate for internal training needs. In the event that you do need to start from scratch, however, think about these questions as you select a web-conferencing vendor:

- What is the budget for your online implementation?
- How technical is the company and staff?
- Will there be firewall issues, or will antivirus software be a factor?
- How many participants will you have at one time?
- Will you need a separate conference calling feature? Do you need voice over Internet protocol, or the routing of voice conversations over the Internet or through any other Internet-protocol-based network?
- Do you want to be able to record the content for use with future trainees?
- Is the bandwidth of your network sufficient enough to transmit the training quickly and reliably to all participants in real time?

On-the-Job Training

Although formal new hire training courses, whether online or offline, are not standard operating procedure for all organizations, on-the-job training certainly is. On-the-job training, also known as OJT or side-by-side training, involves having a new employee work directly with someone who already performs that function and practice relevant tasks in a supervised environment. Although this type of training is less structured than formal coursework, it's also less expensive, requires less ongoing maintenance, and has less of an impact on daily productivity. It also facilitates the new employee's integration into his department and allows him to get a well-rounded perspective, up front, on all his job duties. Even when formal new hire coursework is available, on-the-job training is usually worked in either as an orientation activity or part of the individual development plan, which we'll discuss in the next section. Figure 8-2 details a process for training a new hire using OJT.

Job Rotation

Many companies I've visited recently have leadership development programs for new talent that center on the concept of job rotation. Job rotation is a training approach that involves moving employees to various departments or areas of a company, or to various jobs within a single department. "PricewaterhouseCoopers is an example of a successful job rotation program," says David Hyatt. "Its Tours of Duty program typically lasts one to two years and allows people to rotate among different PricewaterhouseCoopers consulting teams around the world. Consultants who are on tour are able to enhance the host team's ability to meet its business needs by sharing their knowledge and skills with team members. In the process, consultants develop language skills, experience a foreign culture, and enhance their technical and interpersonal skill sets. As with other training techniques, job rotation is most successful if it is part of an overall career development system that offers employees a variety of job-relevant experiences and opportunities."

Individual Development Plans

Most large organizations have processes for preparing new hire development plans that are tied to a performance management system. But if your operation is new or on the smaller side, you may not have formalized this. To guide the new employee and ensure that she's working at her full potential, you should take the time to develop an initial 90-day training plan as well as a long-term plan. The organizational psychologist Ben Dattner suggests these steps for developing new talent:

- *Define the current role:* Determine competencies for success based on job tasks and responsibilities, trying to draw from your job analysis and description, as described in chapter 1. Establish lines of authority and accountability with supervisors and subordinates.
- *Assess developmental needs:* Determine success factors to be measured by benchmarking. You may be able to document past performance and current skill level by recalling your conversations with the employee's references, or his scores on assessment tests. Identify methods that will isolate and measure the employee's on-the-job performance.

Figure 8-2. On-the-Job Training Chart

Step	Purpose	What to Do
1. Prepare the learner	• To relieve tension. • To establish training base. • To stimulate interest. • To give the trainee confidence in performing the task.	• Put the trainee at ease. • Find out what the trainee already knows about the task. • Relate task to overall objective. • Link task to the trainee's experience. • Make sure the trainee is comfortable to see you perform the task clearly.
2. Present the task	• To make sure the trainee understands what to do and why. • To ensure retention. • To avoid giving the trainee more than he or she can absorb.	• Tell, show, and question carefully and patiently. • Emphasize key points. • Instruct clearly and completely one step at a time. • Keep your words to a minimum. Stress action words.
3. Try out trainee's performance	• To be sure the trainee has learned the correct method. • To prevent poor habit development. • To be sure the trainee knows how the task is to be performed and why. • To test the trainee's knowledge. • To avoid putting the trainee on the job prematurely.	• Observe the trainee perform the task without your instruction. If the trainee commits a substantial error, repeat step 2. • Upon correct completion of the task, have the trainee repeat the task. This time, the trainee should explain the task as he or she performs it. • Ask questions to ensure that the key points are understood.
4. Follow-up	• To show your confidence in the trainee. • To give the trainee self-confidence. • To be sure the trainee has been trained properly. • To foster a feeling of self-sufficiency in the trainee.	• Make favorable comments about trainee's current work and progress to date. • Let the trainee work independently. • Frequently monitor the trainee's work. • Gradually reduce trainee monitoring.

This chart was provided by Entrepreneur Magazine (2007).

●   *Coach and train:* Explore the new employee's goals and prioritize her strengths and weaknesses. Work with her to identify where she needs or wants to be in comparison to where she is currently and select two to three areas of focus for development. Then, implement an action plan that will address her specific goals, sustain her motivation over time, and allow you to gather feedback and track progress at regular intervals. "Setting up a schedule for future 360 reviews and development plans based on feedback from future assessments signals an immediate investment in the new hire," agrees Chris Musselwhite, president and CEO of Discovery Learning. "Plus, it gives the person firm dates at which she is going to be assessed on her performance, and provides timely feedback to the organization on whether the person is working out or not."

For a great many new hires, opportunity for advancement is also an important consideration. "Most employees want to know what their potential for growth is within a company, so the sooner you have the discussion with your employee the better the situation and the more likely the employee is to remain loyal to the company," says Marlon Doles, senior human resources manager at Campbell Soup Company. "When putting together your initial development strategy, you should also talk to the new hire about growth opportunities and plan ways to revisit the issue throughout the year."

Devising a career ladder for your new hire can prove helpful in this regard. A career ladder, says Harvard Business Essentials (2002) in *Hiring and Keeping the Best People*, is a logical series of stages that move an employee progressively through more challenging and responsible positions. You can use it by systematically analyzing a person's current level of skills and experience and matching those against what's needed at the next step of the ladder. Gaps between what the person has and what he needs are addressed through a plan that involves a combination of formal training, special assignments, and regular mentoring by a respected superior. Career ladders are most effective when they avoid plateaus. If circumstances bar a promising employee's vertical advancement for the foreseeable future, you should find some type of lateral assignment that will engage his interest and provide learning experiences.

The way you document all this information is up to you and may depend at least in part on a system your organization already has in place. The most important factor is to make sure you develop the plan collaboratively with the new hire and put it in writing. "So often people fail in being explicit about expectations, and are then disappointed in new hire performance," says Francie Dalton, president of Dalton Alliances. "This is frustrating for both parties, and is easily avoided if performance metrics are established up front. Those who are the internal customers of this position should participate in creating the content of the training programs and the measures by which competence should be determined."

Mentoring Programs

I swear by mentoring as one of the best ways to assimilate new employees into an organization, teach them what they need to know to be productive, and send the message that you think they're important and care about their growth. In this section, we talk about how to get a formal mentoring program off the ground and how to ensure the most fruitful one-to-one mentoring relationships.

Linda Phillips-Jones (2002a), cofounder of the Mentoring Group, says that before implementing a formal mentoring initiative, you should consider how much support mentoring has from executives and employees, the time and resources people have to spend, and the overall health of the organization. These steps, she says, are preparation musts:

- Plan ahead. Take several months to plan your initiative and get senior stakeholder buy-in.
- Link goals to the mission and values of your organization. As the organizational and mentoring expert Kathy Kram has emphasized, mentoring efforts that aren't linked to the goals of the organization will not be taken seriously and will fail.
- Don't do everything yourself. Create a dynamic task force that's excited about mentoring. Be sure everyone has a key role and set of tasks.
- Don't reinvent the wheel. Good materials for designing programs and for training mentors and mentees exist. Check out listings on the web. Consider bringing in one or more consultants to help you think through your strategy, train everyone, and evaluate the impact of the mentoring effort.
- Provide structure. If you opt for a program with mentor-mentee pairs (or mentoring circles), plan a great deal of structure. Have a formal application

process, clear roles for participants, formalized training, materials, and scheduled ongoing activities. You can always loosen up, but it's harder to tighten up if a formal program begins with a too-casual approach.

- Start small. You want to be successful in all respects, so focus a pilot effort on a group that is likely to do well. Two good targets are new hires and budding leaders.
- Evaluate everything you do. Don't wait until the year is over and try to pull together some results to decide if you'll do it again. Go beyond feel good data that say the training was enjoyable. Try to get some baseline data before you begin on mentees' competencies, knowledge, attendance, and satisfaction with the organization.

Selecting appropriate mentors for your program is one of the most critical parts of your process. According to *Hiring and Keeping the Best People*, you should seek mentor candidates who can empathize with an employee facing special challenges, have a nurturing attitude, exemplify the best of the company's culture, and have rock-solid links to the organization. I also believe that the best mentors tend to be people who are just a few years ahead of the mentee on the corporate ladder, because they can relate to the mentee's current situation but also have enough perspective to provide concrete and workable advice.

Once you have your volunteers and are ready to begin, get your mentor-mentee relationships off on the right foot by advocating the Mentoring Group's process (Phillips-Jones 2002b):

- *Build the relationship.* The focus here is on getting to know each other and establishing a foundation of trust. Begin to explore the experiences and goals of both the mentee and the mentor.
- *Negotiate agreements.* After you've become acquainted, you're ready to create a set of operating agreements for your mentoring relationship. For example, define your role as a mentor or mentee, determine your schedule and meeting logistics, and clarify any limitations or preferences in the relationship.
- *Develop the mentee.* During this step, the mentoring partners will choose objectives to reach the mentee's goals, select development activities to achieve these objectives, and maintain regular contact with each other.

- *End the relationship.* A formal ending prevents the relationship from dwindling without focus or disintegrating from inactivity. It also gives each mentoring partner a needed sense of closure and a transition into a less formal partnership or a new mentoring arrangement. It's an excellent time to evaluate your work together, celebrate your accomplishments, and plan for the future.

For an example of how a successful mentoring program can work, see the Southwest Airlines Case Study sidebar.

Southwest Airlines Case Study

Before flyers can interview to become a Southwest Airlines pilot, they must have a minimum number of flying hours behind them. To help them as they accrue their hours, they're invited to form a mentoring relationship with an experienced Southwest pilot. "We want these recruits to hear stories from pilots who have been in their shoes before," says Lilah Steen. She and Amy Webb manage the Take Off mentoring program for the flight operations recruiting team in Southwest's People (human relations) Department.

"As they gain their hours, it helps them to have a point of contact at Southwest to get some advice and ask questions like, 'You've been down this route before. How did you get where you are?'" Steen says.

Southwest wants to ensure that it will have enough qualified pilots to meet its hiring needs for years to come. The airline currently employs 4,100 pilots. "We felt it would help to establish relationships with people while they were in school or gaining the time needed to apply here," Steen says. "About 50 to 60 pilots have volunteered to tell the mentees more about Southwest and answer their questions about applying here and what a career with Southwest is like." Another goal of the mentoring program is to reach out to women and minorities who are interested or just getting started in aviation careers. "We want to supply them the information they need to help them be successful," Webb says.

"This idea actually started at the top of our organization and had been talked about for quite a while," Webb says. "So the top executives were definitely on board with it from the beginning."

(continued on the next page)

Southwest Airlines Case Study (continued)

Much of the credit for the program's success goes to the pilots who serve as mentors. "We couldn't do it without the buy-in of the pilots," Steen says. "They've been very enthusiastic about this program. I just got an email from one of our mentees letting us know she was going to go flying with her mentor and the mentor had been wonderful."

"When we launched our program, we sent a memo to our pilots asking them to sign up if they were interested in being a mentor." Steen says. "To those who showed an interest, we sent some talking points so they could answer questions about the goal of the program and what's required of participants."

Potential mentees may learn about the Take Off program at job fairs, but another way many of them hear about it is from Southwest pilots. "The pilots love to talk up the program," Webb says. "If they meet someone who's interested, the pilots let that person know how to get in touch with us and become involved. One of our goals is to get information on our website so people can find out about it that way, too."

Mentees who already know a Southwest pilot are matched with that pilot if possible. Otherwise, Steen matches the mentee with a pilot who lives in the same area. "Then the pair takes it from there," she says. "I provide the pilot with information on mentoring and the background of the mentee, and then we give a lot of leeway on how the mentor and mentee want to build their relationship. Some prefer to meet person-to-person, while others like to communicate by email or phone, whatever works best for the pair." Once the mentee reaches the number of flying hours needed to interview, they'll be phased out of the mentoring program.

"We'd like to find out what value the mentees are gaining from mentoring when they come in to interview, but it's still too early in the program for us to do that," Webb says. "We also hope to have an annual open house where our mentors can meet each other and talk about the program."

This case study was provided by MediaPro, Inc.

Making It Happen

Having appropriate processes in place that enable people to develop their skills in the right way increases competitive ability, motivation, and your company's reputation. Take these steps to improve your training efforts:

- Zero in on the most critical questions about your business processes, your employees' skill acquisition, and the training tactics that will handily address both.
- Use tactics such as formal courses, on-the-job training, and job rotation to provide new hires with information about the organization's policies, resources, performance expectations, and necessary skills.
- Talk with new employees about growth opportunities and devise career ladders for them.
- Recruit your organization's most talented and loyal individuals to serve as mentors for new hires.

Achieve Long-Term Retention: Combat Wandering Eyes by Motivating People to Stick Around

.... **In this chapter, you'll learn to** ....

- offer growth opportunities and incentives that won't break the bank
- teach new supervisors to be successful in their roles
- look out for your top performers by carefully managing staffing issues and work/life balance and by regularly soliciting feedback
- consider your workplace's generational mix and design retention strategies accordingly.

Employee retention is the single most critical factor for business success, according to a recent *Entrepreneur Magazine* (2006) and PricewaterhouseCoopers Entrepreneurial Challenges Survey. Unfortunately, changes in the world of work are making retention more challenging than ever. "The trend toward free agency, the dissolving employer-employee contract, an intensifying need for technical skills, and a growth in Internet recruiting are making it easier for people to learn about and apply for jobs at other companies," says Harvard Business Essentials (2002) in *Hiring and Keeping the Best People*.

As we talked about in earlier chapters, losing employees after you've undertaken the time and resources to train them greatly affects your organization's productivity—and costs a bundle. Clearly, all the strategies we've discussed so far contribute to increasing retention, especially setting level employee expectations during the recruitment and selection process and getting them off to a strong start with effective new hire orientations and thoughtfully conceived training programs. Now we turn to other best practices to help you ensure that your best people stay put, including growth opportunities and incentives, work/life balance, and supervisor musts. We also address some ways to better manage your workforce to boost retention, including keeping in mind generational differences.

Let Incentives Do the Talking

Chapter 8 addressed the importance of establishing performance objectives and setting up a customized growth plan that can help the individual get to the next rung on his or her career ladder. These activities, of course, are critical to retention, because a stalemated career is a common reason for the decision to leave an organization.

Promotions are obviously beneficial in demonstrating to employees that the company understands and appreciates their contributions. But given that it's impossible to promote everyone all the time, what other incentives can you provide? The ones that first come to mind are financial. In terms of compensation, strive to bring the salaries of all your employees up to industry standards and eliminate internal pay disparities. According to Christopher Pritchard (2007) in his book *101 Strategies for Recruiting Success*, you can also use long-term financial incentives such as year-end bonuses, 401(k) matching schedules, additional vacation days, and stock purchase programs. Financial rewards should be tied to future payout schedules.

Employees also like to know they have the option to try a different type of job without leaving the organization. In *Hiring and Keeping the Best People*, Harvard Business Essentials (2002) advocates making sure your free-ranging talent is aware of the opportunities that exist within your own company. Have an internal, online job search tool that conveys the message that it's OK to look for another job within the company. Make the tool functional and fun to use by including anecdotes about people who have transferred and the ability to send out notifications, and allow people concerned with confidentiality to use a noncompany email address. You can also provide additional challenges by appointing a superstar employee to a special committee or task force.

Other incentives include perks like gift certificates or meals out, and "employee of the month" type programs that facilitate group or organization-wide recognition. If an individual successfully finishes a project, put an announcement on the intranet or in the e-newsletter and plan an impromptu celebration. "Employees will feel part of the group with recognition of their first success, so plan group meetings for communicating progress and fostering idea exchanges," says Chip Taylor, project director at TWC Group. You can also build in opportunities to acknowledge everyone on the team by writing down the dates of your employees' birthdays and work anniversaries and taking time out of the business day to observe them.

Supervisor Musts

In my meetings with human resources executives and hiring managers, poor supervisor-employee relationships are cited as a major barrier to retention. Employees may not be able to accurately determine why they're unhappy in a job, and it's often easiest to blame the situation on the boss.

Organizations unknowingly contribute to this problem by failing to show new supervisors the ropes. "Management training is often viewed as a luxury, and it often the first line item to be cut when budgets become strained," says Francie Dalton, president of Dalton Alliances. "Employers must wake up *now* and realize that retention is a strategic necessity and that managerial skill is *crucial* to retention." If they are to be successful in their roles, newly minted supervisors must set clear expectations, encourage accountability, deliver constructive criticism, learn to assess the motivations of their team members, and manage an array of personal styles. This is not easy, and it doesn't happen overnight or without support. Whether it's developed in house or via a consultancy, a formal management course should be a part of every organization's training repertoire.

Supervisors with an eye on retention encourage mutual respect, autonomy, and information sharing among the team. "If you want to make your employees feel valued, inspire their passions and encourage them to make their own decisions," says

Richard Chang of Richard Chang Associates. "They need to know that you trust their judgment and believe in their ideas." Such managers also try to create the type of workplace culture that's most appealing to their employees. "For example," says Harvard Business Essentials, "if you have young, high-energy employees who want a more informal culture, perhaps relax the dress code. To that point, managers must be visible symbols of the culture they aim to promote. If the supervisor says 'let's be casual' but still wears suits every day, anyone who aspires to being at the top will keep on wearing a suit."

Keeping the lines of communication open is also critical for retention-minded managers. Good methods for formal performance reviews are discussed briefly in the sidebar on performance reviews, and figure 9-1 gives a sample review. You should also take advantage of opportunities for your employees to let you know how you're doing. "Three-hundred-sixty-degree reviews are an excellent addition to the development process because they show a manager how he is perceived by others, providing invaluable feedback before bad habits and perceptions form that can't be changed," says Chris Musselwhite, president and CEO of Discovery Learning.

High-Impact Performance Reviews

The mere thought of giving a performance review still makes some want to run for the hills, but a greater focus on constructive feedback and proactive planning have made this annual or semiannual exercise a lot less painful than it has been in the past. Instead of feeling obligated to address the employee with a litany of her shortcomings, the 21st-century manager uses the review as just one meeting in a series of regular get-togethers to chat about progress on previously determined objectives and devise strategies for meeting current challenges. In this type of review, there are no surprises, because the supervisor and the report have been discussing these issues all along. If your organization doesn't already have a performance review methodology in place, here are six simple steps to follow in preparing for and delivering one:

Step 1: Make sure your chosen review process is legal. In *Performance Planning and Appraisal*, Patricia King (1984) says that performance appraisals must be based on a thorough analysis of the job; standardized for all employees; not biased against any race, color, sex, religion, or nationality; and performed by people who have adequate knowledge of the person or job.

Step 2: Develop your documentation. If you are putting together an appraisal form from scratch, you'll first want to devise a rating scale—perhaps from 1 to 4, with 1 being "outstanding" and 4 being "needs improvement." Include established objectives and job responsibilities from your job description and analysis, as well as the measured outcomes. You can also incorporate a section for assessment of important qualities such as productivity, dependability, and initiative. The last section should have room for the next year's development plan, with accompanying objectives and actions, and the report should end with signature lines for both the manager and the employee. For a visual representation of a sample performance review form, see figure 9-1.

Step 3: Schedule the in-person meeting. Ideally, formal performance reviews should be held every six months, but if your employee is new, you may want to have one after the first 90 days. Tell the report about the review, and instruct her on what she'll need to do to prepare.

Step 4: Organize your thoughts for the appraisal form. "Be sure you are familiar with the job requirements and have sufficient contact with the employee to be making valid judgments," says Carter McNamara of Authenticity Consulting. "Use examples to avoid hearsay, and address behaviors, not personality characteristics." Take out last year's review, if there is one, and note what was achieved. If the employee regularly interacts with others, think about soliciting their feedback as well. Expect him to broach the subject of career growth and compensation, and think about what you'll say when the time comes.

Step 5: Conduct the review. Start off by explaining the purpose of the review (that is, to exchange feedback and to discuss the status of previously determined objectives, outline new goals, and formulate or update the development plan). Let the employee comment on her performance first. Listen carefully and then respond with a mix of constructive criticism and positive feedback. If a disagreement comes up, try to remain objective and keep your defensiveness to a minimum. Write down any agreements made about future goals and action plans while they're still fresh in your mind. Leave time at the end of the meeting for the employee to ask questions and air issues, and make sure she understands what will be expected over the next year.

Step 6: Finalize and sign the appraisal form. Add comments to your portion of the form based on the in-person discussion, and have the employee add his thoughts as well. Both of you should sign the completed form and commit to revisiting the development plan every few months.

Figure 9-1. Sample Performance Review

Date _____

Prepared by_____

Title _____

Department_____

Employee Name and Title _____

This review covers the period from_____to_____

Document the employee's performance using the following ratings.

Performance Rating Definitions

1 — CLEARLY OUTSTANDING: Repeatedly exceeds, by a significant degree, *most* of the major requirements of the position, while maintaining fully satisfactory performance in the remaining duties. This rating usually includes the top 10 percent of the workforce.

2 — ABOVE EXPECTATIONS: Exceeds, by a significant degree, *some* of the major requirements of the job while maintaining fully satisfactory performance in the remaining duties.

3 — MEETS EXPECTATIONS: Performance results are satisfactory in all aspects of the job.

4 — NEEDS IMPROVEMENT: Improvement is needed in one or more performance areas. Results are less than normally expected.

ACCOMPLISHMENTS

Established Objectives:

Major Responsibilities and Projects:

Outcomes:

PERSONAL ASSESSMENT

Quality of Work: Consider the accuracy, thoroughness, and presentation of the work performed.

PERSONAL ASSESSMENT (continued)

Productivity: Look at whether the employee routinely meets established deadlines and produces satisfactory work.

Interpersonal Skills: Consider how well the employee works with others, resolves problems, and assists others.

Dependability: Look at the employee's consistency in producing good-quality work. Also note the employee's attendance record.

Initiative: Consider the employee's willingness to seek out additional responsibilities.

Job Knowledge: Look at the extent to which the employee applies his/her knowledge of workplace technologies, methods, and skills.

Overall Evaluation: Select the one rating that best describes the employee's performance throughout the review period:

- Clearly outstanding
- Above expectations
- Meets expectations
- Needs improvement.

DEVELOPMENT PLAN

Development Objectives:

Actions Anticipated:

Employee's Feedback:

Manager's Signature_____

Employee's Signature _____

Date _____

"Stay interviews," or meetings in which managers ask current employees how they feel about the organization, the work environment, and their current level of job satisfaction, are also a great way for supervisors to identify potential retention problems early. In addition to scheduling these meetings roughly every six months, Harvard Business Essentials says that you should be on the lookout for signs of defection, including a change in behavior, a decline in performance, sudden complaints from a person who's not a complainer, wistful references to other companies, or withdrawal behavior. Arrange to meet with the employee as soon as possible, and use probing questions to identify the source of the problem. Indicate that you value him or her as an employee and ask how you can work together to create a better work experience.

Walking the Tightrope of Work versus Life

Now that I'm a manager, I've found that it's partly up to me to ensure that my reports have good work/life balance. I've seen other supervisors ignore this issue, expecting that work should be the only thing that matters to employees, and as a result, the department has a revolving door. Here are some of the methods I've used:

- Make expectations clear, while giving reports the freedom to achieve tasks in the timeframe and manner that works best for them. This means that if it's the day before a holiday and all the work is done, I might suggest they take off early.
- Help them find the time to undertake activities that are personally meaningful to them, like going to a friend's wedding the weekend before a project is due, or signing up for a creative writing seminar that takes them out of the office for an hour each week.
- Give employees laptops, cell phones, and BlackBerries to make it easier for them to balance the needs of work and family. Again, what's important is that the work gets done, not whether it's completed in the office during the hours of 9 to 5.

Other measures that organizations are putting in place to encourage work/life balance are flexible schedules and telecommuting. Flextime arrangements such as reduced, part-time, or compressed schedules (for example, the employee works 40 hours from Monday to Thursday and takes Friday off) are becoming more common and accepted as companies acknowledge the struggles families with two working parents face in caring for children. Flexible scheduling sometimes incorporates job sharing, in which a full-time position is split between two people.

According to Harvard Business Essentials' (2002) *Hiring and Keeping the Best People*, telework offers cost savings and benefits, including lower real estate costs, greater employee productivity, greater employee loyalty and job satisfaction, and lower turnover. However, the book wisely advises that before implementing telecommuting, you consider these questions:

- Which jobs are appropriate for telework?
- What are the legal, regulatory, insurance, and technology issues?
- How will you supervise teleworkers to ensure accountability?
- Will employees worry that telework will negatively affect their chances for promotions and other recognition?

Looking for Your Top Performers

Retention is also easier when you look at your workforce or department from a big picture perspective and make sure you take care of those employees who add the most value. Deciding who these people are is somewhat subjective, but Harvard Business Essentials (2002) describes them as those who provide formal or informal leadership, consistently produce excellent results, contribute valuable and practical new ideas, require little to no supervision, facilitate the work of others, have unique knowledge or skills that would be costly and time consuming to replace, and could do the organization harm if they defected to competitors. These are the employees who should receive the lion's share of retention resources and attention. Besides what we've talked about already, here are some of the things you can do to look out for your top performers:

- Take a fresh look at jobs that might be considered boring, repetitive, and isolating, and make an effort to redesign them. Customize jobs so that they meet the needs of your best employees' individual situations, take advantage of their talents, and provide variety and new challenges.
- Watch for burnout, or work exhaustion, which, says Harvard Business Essentials, occurs when people feel that they have more stress than support in their work lives. Conflicting demands, interpersonal conflict, and failure to achieve real success can cause burnout and result in reduced

self-esteem, a decline in feelings of competence and achievement, and a detached or negative approach to colleagues and clients.

- Anticipate staffing needs ahead of time and make sure you provide enough training for employees to do their jobs efficiently and well. Monitor what's on the plates of your top employees and meet with them periodically to ensure that they don't feel overwhelmed or underappreciated.

- Ask your employees for their opinions through one-to-one meetings, feedback sessions, or even surveys. Then take action on their ideas. "Asking for input and doing nothing with it damages your credibility as a leader," says David Hyatt, president of CorVirtus. "Simply attempting to improve the employee experience will go a long way in the eyes of your people."

Also, because the mere presence of poor performers affects the retention of your best people, you must take action to weed these people out. Work with other supervisors to execute probationary plans and timeframes for improvement or dismissal.

To conclude the discussion on retention, please have a look at the case study on TalentKeepers, which illustrates the financial benefits of reducing turnover.

Managing Baby Boomers, Generation Xers, and More

Considering that there are currently four different generations in the workforce, a frequently asked question in my seminars is how managers need to relate to members of each generation specifically. In *Managing the Generation Mix*, Carolyn Martin and Bruce Tulgan (2006) define the generations as follows:

- *Schwarzkopfers:* Born before 1946, and named after war hero General Norman Schwarzkopf, their strengths are loyalty, dependability, responsibility, altruism, and a strong work ethic. Other generations can count on these seasoned workers for everything from historical perspective to an important document. Their attitude is "take charge" and "do what's right."

- *Baby Boomers:* The huge Baby Boom generation, born between 1946 and 1964, experienced a child-centered upbringing, a focus on individuality and youth, and a distrust of anyone in authority. Older Boomers admit they're competitive and self-centered, but they have a strong commitment to the mission of their organizations. Younger Boomers see themselves as cautiously loyal and more realistic about life and work.

TalentKeepers Case Study

One of the largest global package delivery and shipping firms was experiencing high turnover in its U.S. sales and services force of nearly 1,000 representatives, costing the firm productivity, lost sales, and a drop in customer satisfaction.

This organization is a global leader in international express services, overland transport, and air freight. It is also one of the world's leaders in ocean freight and contract logistics. It offers a full range of customized solutions, from express document shipping to supply chain management. It operates in over 220 countries and has more than 250,000 employees.

The company had completed a major acquisition in an attempt to broaden its product range and gain a competitive advantage. However, as is often the case following mergers and acquisitions, it was not gaining the expected synergies, and customer service levels and sales were declining in large part due to significant turnover among its experienced sales and services staff.

Following a turnover cost analysis, the company determined that the impact of losing an experienced sales or services person averaged $57,200 in direct costs and an estimated $171,600 in indirect costs, such as lost sales, shipping errors, and customer complaints. Senior management made reducing turnover an urgent matter along with improving customer service.

Working with TalentKeepers, the organization began by gathering important metrics on the cost of losing a sales representative, plus turnover rates by region and sales manager. This information was used to quantify the overall cost of the problem as well as to determine the return-on-investment opportunity for reducing the unwanted attrition. In addition, through the use of TalentKeepers' TalentWatch survey, sales representatives were asked about the organizational issues (such as pay and benefits), job issues (tasks and schedules), and leader issues (trust, fair treatment, and being flexible) that were influencing workers to join, stay, and leave the organization.

Opportunities were identified and acted upon in each factor (organizational, job, and leader) to increase their influence on sales representatives to stay. Frontline sales leaders were found to have the strongest influence on the stay/leave decisions of sales representatives. Leaders also highly influenced the degree of trust the sales representatives placed in the organization. Consequently, all sales leaders were trained to improve their trust building and communication skills using TalentKeepers' Retention Leadership Series.

(continued on next page)

> **TalentKeepers Case Study (*continued*)**
>
> In 12 months, sales and services attrition decreased by 29 percent, which resulted in a significant cost savings, plus increased sales performance and customer satisfaction. The company estimates the reduced turnover saved it $4.6 million in direct costs and another $13.9 million savings in indirect costs. The total savings were over $18.5 million.
>
> *This case study was provided by TalentKeepers (2004).*

- *Generation Xers:* These independent, ambitious "go getters," born between 1965 and 1977, are accustomed to taking care of themselves. Not obsessed with climbing the corporate ladder, these free agents are energetic, creative, and adaptable as they make lifestyle choices that contribute to their wellness, happiness, and health.
- *Generation Yers/Millennials:* Born after 1977, Yers are the most outspoken and empowered of all the generations. Influenced by education-minded boomer parents and fueled by their facility with technology, Yers are poised to be lifelong learners. They're socially conscious, have high expectations of organizations, and are constantly looking for ways to improve how things are done.

Managing and retaining members of each of these generations is a task unto itself, and Martin and Tulgan suggest that you employ different strategies according to the age of your employees. Top-line recommendations for each generation include the following (Figure 9-2 offers a helpful worksheet for planning your generational management strategy).

For Schwarzkopfers:

- Ask Schwarzkopfers about the work itself during one-to-one conversations about job satisfaction.
- Encourage "making the call." Support these experienced people in using their own judgment in making business decisions.
- Don't allow Schwarzkopfers to coast. Rigorously offer feedback and base rewards on performance.
- Create knowledge transfer programs, for example, by having a go-to list of Schwarzkopfer experts whom younger workers can contact for information.

Figure 9-2. Generational Management Strategy Worksheet

Think about the Schwarzkopfers, Baby Boomers, Generation Xers, and Generation Yers/Millennials who you manage. List your employees according to their generation. How do they exemplify the experiences, attitudes, behaviors, and expectations of their generation? What challenges do they present right now? Ask yourself how you can address these challenges to become a more effective manager.

Generation	Experiences, attitudes, behaviors, expectations	Challenges	Your actions

This worksheet was provided by Carolyn Martin and Bruce Tulgan (2006) in Managing the Generation Mix.

For Baby Boomers:

- Give Boomers recognition. This means honoring their opinions, knowledge, potential, and contributions and finding appropriate ways to reward them.
- Self-improvement is a major Boomer aspiration. Become a coach who challenges boomers to grow, and encourage them to mentor the next generation of leaders.
- Let them try out new ideas. Offer them the flexibility and authority to experiment, and support them if they fail.
- Help bridge the team/individual divide, because Boomers are driven by conflicting impulses between doing what's best for the team and distinguishing themselves.

For Generation Xers:

- Provide them with opportunities to amass marketable skills and experience. To Xers, training equals security.
- Place value on career development opportunities, and increase Xers' spheres of responsibility as warranted. Make sure you offer compensation commensurate with contribution.
- Flexible work arrangements are important to Xers, who first pioneered the concept of work/life balance and now have families to think about.
- Provide access to decision makers. When in need, Xers want to get information, resources, and answers quickly.

For Generation Yers/Millennials:

- Get to know Yers and their individual capabilities. Show them you genuinely care about their success.
- Establish coaching relationships, positioning yourself as a dynamic source of learning, tools, and resources.
- Treat Yers as colleagues rather than "know-nothing kids." Customize schedules and position special assignments as rewards for high performance.
- Consistently provide constructive feedback. Let Yers know what they're doing well, and how they can improve *today*.

Regardless of your unique mix of employees, however, it's imperative that you facilitate strong communication across generations and among individual team members. Consistently tuning into the needs and wants of all of your employees will make them much more likely to stay.

Making It Happen

Losing employees after you've undertaken the time and resources to train them greatly affects your organization's success. Encourage your best people to stay put by doing the following:

- Strive to bring the salaries of all your employees up to industry standards, implement nonfinancial perks, and facilitate internal transfers.
- Provide managerial training in which supervisors learn to set clear expectations, encourage accountability, and assess motivations.
- Promote work/life balance by giving employees the freedom to achieve tasks in the timeframe and manner that works best for them.
- Understand generational differences and customize retention practices according to your group's age mix.

Afterword

In the last nine chapters, we've outlined a proven process for keeping your organization on top and combating the "brain drain" that will take place as the Baby Boomers begin to retire in the next few years. We've discussed

- how to create accurate job analyses and descriptions
- how to search for talent in the right places
- how to conduct screening, background research, and assessments
- how to interview effectively
- how to manage a candidate's acceptance and orientation
- how to develop training and growth plans
- how to retain employees over the long haul.

If you think you don't have time for this, consider the negative effects of hiring a single wrong employee:

> Wrong hiring decision → Poorly performing employee → Misallocated management time and resources → Neglect of business and other employees → Low morale among top performers → Rapid turnover → Decrease in organizational effectiveness and customer satisfaction.

Financially speaking, the costs of turnover are steep. For example, John Bishop, founder of Accent on Success, tells us of a Saint Louis photocopier company that figured its first year cost to train a copier repair person to be in excess of $63,000. That figure included salary, training costs, travel, road time with the supervisor, advertising for the position, and overtime for other repair people to cover the area until a new person could be hired.

Similarly, according to Bishop, the Rutgers University Graduate School of Business estimates that the turnover cost for a nonprofessional position is 1.5 times that person's annual salary, while the cost for a professional position is as much as 2 times that person's salary. The question is, would your colleagues look at the hiring process differently if they knew the impact it would have on their budgets?

But, you say, how can we prove that implementing this process will prevent us from making wrong hiring decisions and increasing our turnover? Consider research from CorVirtus, which found that a standardized selection system reduced employee turnover by 20 to 60 percentage points. Although this reduction in turnover is a positive outcome in and of itself, it often leads to other positive outcomes such as improved employee performance (between 10 and 15 percent) and increased productivity (for hourly employees, as much as $3 per employee).

The impending labor shortage means that the time to address your hiring issues is now. And when you take a step back from all the steps and instructions and advice, you'll probably realize that many of the best practices for recruitment and retention aren't terribly complicated or difficult to implement. It's simply a matter of sitting down and prioritizing a winning mix of initiatives that will be most relevant to your business objectives and best safeguard your organization's future: your people. Best of luck!

References

Beck & Tysver PLLC. 2007. Confidentiality Agreement. *Bitlaw: A Resource on Technology Law*. http://www.bitlaw.com.

Business Owner's Toolkit. 2007. Avoiding Unintended Hiring Contracts. http://www.toolkit.com.

Cullen, Lisa Takahashi. 2006. Getting Wise to Lies. *Time*, April 24. http://www.time.com.

DeCotiis, Thomas. 2006. Use Reliable Background Checkers to Fish Criminals and Liars Out of Your Hiring Pool. http://www.corvirtus.com.

Development Dimensions International. 2004. Client Successes: Innovex. http://www.ddiworld.com.

Entrepreneur Magazine. 2006. Entrepreneurial Challenges Survey Results. http://www.entrepreneur.com.

———. 2007. On-the-Job Training Chart. http://www.entrepreneur.com.

Flynn, Gillian. 2002. E-Recruiting Ushers in Legal Dangers. *Workforce Management*, April. http://www.workforce.com.

Franklin, Maren. 2005. A Guide to Job Analysis. *ASTD Infoline*, issue 0506.

Gala, Christa. 2006. Don't Be Desperate. *QSR*. http://www.qsrmagazine.com.

Giordani, Pattie. 2005. Y Recruiting: New Generation Inspires New Methods. *NACE Journal* 65, no. 4: 23–25.

Gorman, Carol Kinsey. 2006. Generation Y: The Millennials: Ready or Not, Here They Come. *NAS Insights*. http://www.nasrecruitment.com.

Handler, Charles A., and Mark C. Healy. 2006. Results from the 4th Annual Rocket-Hire Online Screening and Assessment Usage Survey. http://www.rocket-hire.com.

Harvard Business Essentials. 2002. *Hiring and Keeping the Best People*. Boston: Harvard Business School Press.

References

Heathfield, Susan. 2005. Updated Job Offer Letter. http://humanresources.about.com.

———. 2007a. Tips for a Better New Employee Orientation. http://humanresources.about.com.

———. 2007b. Top Ten Ways to Turn Off a New Employee. http://humanresources.about.com.

———. 2007c. Tips for Determining a Motivating Salary. http://humanresources.about.com.

Intulogy. 2007a. Case Study: Call Center Training. http://www.intulogy.com.

———. 2007b. Instructional Design. http://www.intulogy.com.

Johnson, Leanne, and Roberta Westwood. 2002. Take Orientation Online. *ASTD Infoline*, issue 0210.

King, Patricia. 1984. *Performance Planning and Appraisal*. New York: McGraw Hill.

Kinsey, Eugene E. 2007. Employee Non-Compete Agreement. http://www.kinseylaw.com.

Martin, Carolyn, and Bruce Tulgan. 2006. *Managing the Generation Mix*. Amherst, MA: HRD Press.

MediaPro. 2007. Case Study: Southwest Airlines. http://www.mediapro.com.

Meth, Simon. 2007. How to Stay No. *SittingXlegged Blog*. www.ere.net/blogs/SittingXlegged.

Musselwhite, Chris. 2007. Finding the Right Person at the Right Time. http://www.inc.com.

Nolo. 2007. Written Employment Contracts: Pros and Cons. http://www.nolo.com.

Phillips-Jones, Linda. 2002a. Getting a Mentoring Program off the Ground. http://www.mentoringgroup.com.

———. 2002b. A Proven Process for Successful Mentoring. http://www.mentoringgroup.com.

Pritchard, Christopher. 2007. *101 Strategies for Recruiting Success*. New York: AMACOM.

Ringler, James. 2007. Technology and the Hiring Process. http://www.corvirtus.com.

Springer, Steve. 2006. *Stop Hiring Failures*. Charleston, SC: BookSurge.

Sullivan, John. 1998. The New Hire's Orientation Toolkit. Gately Consulting. http://ourworld.compuserve.com/homepages/gately.

TalentKeepers. 2004. Global Shipping and Delivery Giant Nets 29% Reduction in Sales and Service Employee Turnover. http://www.talentkeepers.com.

Uprichard, John. 2006. How to Avoid Making a Panic Hire. http://businessedge.michcpa.org.

Yate, Martin. 2006. *Hiring the Best: Manager's Guide to Effective Interviewing and Recruiting*. Avon, MA: Adams Media.

Suggested Reading

Allen, Michael. 2006. *E-Learning Library: Creating Successful E-Learning: A Rapid System For Getting It Right First Time, Every Time.* New York: Pfeiffer.

Belker, Loren, and Gary Topchik. 2005. *The First-Time Manager.* New York: AMACOM.

Branham, Leigh. 2005. *The 7 Hidden Reasons Employees Leave: How to Recognize the Subtle Signs and Act Before It's Too Late.* New York: AMACOM.

Burgio-Murphy, Andrea, and Mark Murphy. 2006. *The Deadly Sins of Employee Retention.* Charleston, SC: BookSurge.

Charan, Ram. 2007. *Know-How: The 8 Skills That Separate People Who Perform from Those Who Don't.* New York: Crown Business.

Hoevemeyer, Victoria A. 2005. *High-Impact Interview Questions: 701 Behavior-Based Questions to Find the Right Person for Every Job.* New York: AMACOM.

Hunt, Steven. 2007. *Hiring Success: The Art and Science of Staffing Assessment and Employee Selection.* New York: Pfeiffer.

Mazin, Rebecca A., and Shawn A. Smith. 2004. *The HR Answer Book: An Indispensable Guide for Managers and Human Resources Professionals.* New York: AMACOM.

Resto, Chris, Ramit Sethi, and Ian Ybarra. 2007. *Recruit or Die: How Any Business Can Beat the Big Guys in the War for Young Talent.* New York: Portfolio/Penguin.

Smart, Bradford D. 2005. *Topgrading: How Leading Companies Win by Hiring, Coaching, and Keeping the Best People.* New York: Portfolio/Penguin.

Smith, Jim. 2007. *Crash and Learn: 600+ Road Tested Tips to Keep Audiences FIRED UP and ENGAGED!* Alexandria, VA: ASTD Press.

Stolovitch, Harold D., and Erica J. Keeps. 2002. *Telling Ain't Training.* Alexandria, VA: ASTD Press.

Weiss, Donald H. 2004. *Fair, Square & Legal: Safe Hiring, Managing & Firing Practices to Keep You & Your Company Out of Court.* New York: AMACOM.

About the Author

Photograph by Amanda Wells

Alexandra Levit is the founder and president of Inspiration@Work, a career consulting firm. She is a former nationally syndicated career columnist with Tribune Media Services and a current blogger for the international job portal Getthejob.com. She has written several books, including the popular *They Don't Teach Corporate in College: A Twenty-Something's Guide to the Business World* (Career Press, 2004) and *How'd You Score That Gig? A Guide to the Coolest Jobs and How to Get Them* (Random House, 2008). Her career advice has been featured in more than 800 media outlets, including ABC News, Fox News, *The Greg Behrendt Show*, the Associated Press, *USA Today*, the *Wall Street Journal*, the *New York Times*, National Public Radio, *Fortune*, Yahoo, and MSN.

Known as one of the premier career spokespeople of her generation, Levit regularly speaks on workplace issues at corporations and organizations around the country, such as ABN AMRO, Campbell Soup, CIGNA, the Federal Reserve Bank, and Whirlpool. A member of the American Society for Training and Development, she graduated from Northwestern University in 1998 and resides in Chicago with her husband, Stewart. Learn more at www.alexandralevit.com.

Index